CHILD OF THE KING

A JOURNEY OF HOPE – BOOK ONE

K. G. INGRAM

K. G. Ingram

Copyright Page

Copyright © 2022 by **Karen Ingram**

Cover Design by Miblart.com

Child of the King, Journey of Hope, Book One, A Novel

ISBN

979-8-88759-249-7 - paperback

979-8-88759-250-3 ebook

DEDICATION

This book is dedicated to the memory of my dear sister in Christ, Cory Palmer.

To the memory of my wonderful Mother-in-law Marta Bradford who by her example helped to lead me back to Jesus.

ACKNOWLEDGMENTS

I want to ACKNOWLEDGE, with great gratitude, my long-standing friendship with several important people. First, my friends and sisters in Christ, Susan Knutson and Diana Schaefer who kept me focused on the truth of the Bible and for being especially encouraging on this journey.

My daughter Kimberly Sexton who took time out of her busy schedule to help with editing.

I also want to express my gratitude to Gary Knutson, for his knowledge of the Bible and his insight in keeping the content true to biblical principles.

Also, I want to thank James Lewis for sharing his passion for the Lord Jesus Christ, illustrating the Logo and encouraging me as I worked my way through writing this volume.

And to Michael Boskovich, who polished and produced the Final Logo design.

A special thank you to my family and friends for believing in me and the wonderful support and encouragement they have offered.

Pastor Nathan Cherry and Pastor Jay Vincent at Westside Christian Church in Roseville, California, for their timely teaching on the Scriptures of John and Mark which were an invaluable and an inspirational resource.

Finally, I want to acknowledge my Husband Bob for loving me through this process. His encouragement and being by my side helped me to finish what I started.

Introduction

I started this book five years ago while caring for my Mother-In-Law, Marta Bradford. She was an inspiration of what it meant to be a woman of faith.

During that time, I began to wonder what it might have been like to walk with Jesus during His ministry on the earth. God gave me a passion to write this novel and guided me through the entire process. The title came to me first, and the journey began.

Walking with Him through this story, caused me to draw even closer to Him by imagining the encounters that people in that time may have experienced.

My prayer is that those who read this book will get a sense of being in the physical presence of Jesus. Although He is physically gone from this place, He is certainly with us continually through His Holy Spirit. We need only to invite Him into our lives.

Even if one person is inspired by this story, it will be worth all the time and effort that went into it.

A sequel will be forthcoming.

'This is an earthly story with a heavenly message.'

CHAPTER 1

I n Cana, a village in the region of Galilee, lived eleven-year-old Azan, a Jewish boy, and his family. Galilee had thriving villages around the rolling hills where grain, orchards, oil, wine, and fish trades were a way of life. It was the year AD28.

Azan was the oldest of four children. His curly, deep brown hair cascaded to his shoulders. He resembled his mother with olive skin and hazel eyes but had his father's strong build.

They lived in a modest, whitewashed, dried mud-brick home on the outskirts of town. It was a one-story structure with three rooms. There was a living area and two other rooms. One room for the children to sleep in and the other for the parents. The front of the house had a large courtyard that was incased in whitewashed waist-high walls. The home was covered by a wood framed overhang of palm leaves which had fallen from their trees, covering the top to supply shade against the afternoon sun.

Azan woke up to the smell of freshly baked bread. He took a deep breath. *I love the smell of mother's bread.* He came into the room as he was putting his cloak on over his tunic.

"Good morning, Mother. Your bread smells so good. I love waking up to the aroma."

"Good morning, Son. Thank you. Did you sleep well?"

"I did."

"Will you call your brothers and your sister to come and eat?"

"Okay." He started toward their room. *Mother is so loving.* He turned and looked at her with admiration. *I bet in another year, I will be as tall as her.* She sensed him looking at her and turned and smiled at him. Her hazel eyes lit up against her olive-colored skin. She returned to her task. Her long, mahogany brown hair tied back with a leather strap hung down to the middle of her thin back.

Todros was the older of his two younger brothers and had just turned seven. He looked at him sleeping. *Todros is so quiet and reserved. He looks the most like Father with his dark hair, deep brown eyes, and dark skin.*

Then he looked at nine-year-old Dobah. Her long, dark hair was hanging off the bed. *She looks a little like both Father and Mother with her brown eyes and olive skin.* He smiled. *I love how she finds it her mission to boss her brothers around.* He chuckled and acknowledged, *with little success. They ignore her commands, but that doesn't stop her from trying.*

"Wake up, it's time to get up."

Todros groaned and stretched his arms above his head. Dobah opened her eyes, smiled at him, sat up on her bed, and pushed her long, curly hair away from her face. She adored her big brother and looked up to him. He went over to Meir and sat down on the side of his bed and gently rubbed his back. *He is certainly an energetic four-year-old.*

"Meir, time to wake up." He turned toward Azan and opened his eyes.

"Time to get up, Meir. Come on. Let's go eat." *His eyes, hair, and skin color look just like Mother, but his slightly crooked smile looked just like Father.*

Meir rubbed his eyes and then raised his arms. Azan picked him up and carried him to the table. He sat down with him in his lap, and Meir laid his head on his shoulder, trying to wake up.

Mother had the morning meal already laid out. There was piping hot bread in the middle of the table. He inhaled the delightful aroma again. In front of each of them was a bowl of millet porridge. He reached for the small bowl of dates and took a spoonful. Cinnamon and honey were also his favorite addition to his bowl. He took a bunch of grapes from the larger bowl and popped one into his mouth. He offered one to Meir, but he pushed it away.

The oil lamps were still flickering from his mother's early morning activities. His father, Yosef, came in from outside and sat at the head of the table. Azan watched his mother put out each of the three lamps as the sun lit up the room. Meir watched her as she came and sat at the table.

Yosef began with the morning prayer, just like he did every morning, as was the tradition in their home. Yosef was a prominent religious leader in their town, and he took his responsibilities seriously. He was tall and had dark, sun-tanned skin. His deep brown eyes matched his hair, and he had a strong build that was enhanced by his labors.

"When you have eaten and are satisfied, praise the Lord your God for the good land He has given us and for blessing us with His provisions. Amen."

Then he broke the bread and passed it to Heba.

Meir jumped down and went to sit in his usual place next to Mother. She placed a piece of bread in front of him and passed the bread on to Dobah.

"Mother, how is it that you work so hard every day, baking bread, making meals, fetching water from the communal well, grinding grain into flour, and sewing clothes, and you never complain?"

She replied, "I enjoy caring for my family, it does not feel like work. Scripture says to do everything unto the Lord."

She contributed to the household income by selling the tunics, cloaks, belts, and head coverings that she made from fabrics that were bought in Beth Shan. She would sit in the afternoons and hand sew the garments as the children played in the courtyard.

He sat watching her help Meir. *I love my relationship with Mother. We can talk about anything.*

As they ate, Azan asked Yosef, "How long have our ancestors been religious leaders under the Sanhedrin?"

"The men in our ancestry have always strictly followed the Jewish law and traditions and passed it down through the ages. It has been our responsibility to enforce Jewish worship and legislate day-to-day affairs in our town in which we live."

He and Azan had moments when they disagreed, and it put a bit of a strain on their relationship at times, but he loved his father and wanted to please him. Azan was getting older. He had his opinions, and he was not timid in expressing them, and that led to contention between them.

Azan finished eating and said, "Please excuse me. I need to get to school."

Heba reminded him, "I will be at the city center by the well after school. Please meet me there."

"Okay, I'll be there after school lets out."

He grabbed his bag, pulled his head covering over his head, said goodbye, and walked out the door toward the school building with its one-room classroom. As he approached the building, he saw his friend.

"Good morning, Eliah."

"Good morning, Azan."

They went in and sat down. Eight other boys filtered in with their chatter filling the room. The Rabbi stood before them and said, "Let's settle down and pray before we begin."

"Father, we come before You to learn of You. I pray that

these before me will be attentive to the teachings of today. Amen."

Then he opened one of the Scrolls to the Scripture of Deuteronomy and began reading. *'Hear, O Israel! The Lord is our God, the Lord is one! You shall love the Lord your God with all your heart and with all your soul and with all your might. These words, which I am commanding you today, shall be on your heart.'*

The Rabbi then instructed them to take out their tablets and continue working on the assignment given at the beginning of the week. They spent the rest of the morning reading, writing, and studying Scripture. The Rabbi was a short older man in his late-fifties and had white hair and a white beard that rested on his chest.

When inside, he took off his head covering and let it lie around his shoulders over his robe. Azan admired his knowledge and wisdom and aspired to be like him.

∾

It was the end of the week, and school had just let out. Azan called out, "Eliah! Wait up!"

Eliah was a little taller than Azan. He was a year older and was slim with medium dark, shoulder length hair, light skin, and brown eyes. They were like brothers, and they had their moments. But they enjoyed each other's friendship.

He caught up with him.

"Mother will be at the well today. Let's find her."

"Did you bring your sling with you?"

"Yes, it's in my bag. I challenge you to see who can hit the most rocks off the log today."

"You think you can beat me?"

"I guess we'll find out."

They walked the short distance to the center, where Azan sees Dobah directing the children in their activities as usual.

Mother was standing and talking with a group of women near the communal well. She looked up and saw the boys as they approached. She reached into her basket and handed them a bag with bread and fruit and motioned them to go sit and eat, not wanting to interrupt the conversation.

Azan said, "Let's go sit in the shade of the blacksmith shop so we can hear what the older men are talking about today."

They walked over and sat down, leaned back on the building, and took a piece of bread and a hand full of grapes out of the bag.

Joseph, the oldest of the bunch, said, "Did you hear about the man who has been baptizing people in the Jordan River? They say he lives in the wilderness and dresses in camel hair clothes with a leather belt tied around him."

His brother Jacob said, "People are saying he is remarkable, and they are flocking to the Jordan to see and hear him preach. They say he looks and speaks like the prophets of old. It's been over four hundred years since we've had a prophet."

The boys looked at each other and tried to listen more closely to what they were saying. Azan's mother came over to them and said, "When you finish, take this food out to the field for your fathers."

Their fathers owned a vineyard together and raised sheep. The boys finished eating and got up and started off to the vineyard. Eliah jumped up to walk on a rock wall that framed the roadway, trying to balance himself while Azan kicked a rock and yelled, "Ouch!" as he limped a few steps until the pain subsided in his toe. "I should know better than to kick a rock."

Eliah said, "I wonder who that man is they were talking about?"

"I don't know, but he sounds interesting. I wonder why he is baptizing people. Can't you picture him in his hairy camel clothes? I wonder if he *is* a prophet, or even Elijah! Let's see what our fathers know about him."

As they walked the quarter mile, Azan asked Eliah, "Are you

going to the Passover this year? Passover is next month. I know
you went last year. I get to go this year because I will be turning
twelve in a couple of weeks. I can only imagine what it will be
like. What *is* it like to go to the Holy City?"

Eliah said, "The Holy Land is about thirty-seven miles from
Cana. We walked for eight to ten hours each day through
Samaria. It took us four days to get there from here.

"We stopped overnight in Beth-Shan the first night. The
second night we stopped around Shechem. We stayed outside of
Bethel the third night. Normally it is not too safe to go through
Samaria, but with the multitudes of people, the Samaritans tend
to leave the pilgrims alone. But it is an easier walk than going
along the Jordan River. The river road is much rougher and a
longer distance. It could take five to seven days to get to
Jerusalem on that route. But it is a safer route than going
through Samaria."

"I have never been farther than Capernaum or Nazareth.
You said you've been to Beth Shan? Father and I are going to
Beth Shan tomorrow to buy items for Mother. She is helping
with preparations for a wedding. It's for the daughter of one of
her close friends here in town."

"Beth Shan is an exciting place to visit. The marketplace is
larger than ours. But nothing like Jerusalem. We are going to
that wedding also; it should be fun. Father is going to Beth Shan
with your father to buy bulk barley and spices for mother. You
will see how different it is than here in Cana. I didn't know you
were going; I'll ask if I can come also."

"There they are,"—Eliah -pointed out to the vineyard—
"bundling the cuttings."

Azan spoke up for them to hear him. "Mother sent food for
you. Come over and eat."

The men stopped working and walked over to the boys.
They all gathered under the shade of one of the fig trees that
lined the roadway. Yosef took a cloth out of his waistband and
wiped the sweat off his face and neck. "How was school today?"

"We studied language, writing, and practiced reading from the Scrolls. Our Rabbi talked to us about how we should be looking forward to the Kingdom of God. Father, when will the Kingdom of God come?"

"It's not for us to know. Only when it happens will we know."

"We heard the elderly men in town talking about a man in the wilderness baptizing people in the Jordan. Do you know anything about him?"

Medad, Eliah's father, said, "I've heard things in town about this man also. Some are saying he is the resurrected prophet, Elijah. I heard he had provoked the religious leaders because he was challenging their religious authority. That's something they don't take lightly."

Medad is such a kind man. He is taller than Father and thinner. Being out in the sun hasn't left him as dark as father. But they both have dark hair and dark eyes.

Yosef replied, "We have to be watchful for false prophets and stay true to what we believe."

When they had finished eating, the men got up to return to the vineyard.

Yosef told the boys, "The flock is on the hillside just down the road. We'll come for you when we are done for the day."

They jumped up and started walking down the road.

CHAPTER 2

A s they walked along, Azan asked, "Tell me more about the trip to Jerusalem."

"When you go through Samaria, after Beth Shan, the only thing to see out there are stone military posts. There is nothing but the long road. When you get close to Beth Shan, all the area surrounding it is green with crops. Like I said, the marketplace is larger than here. There's merchandise from all over the world."

Azan was excited. "I find Nazareth and Capernaum not much different from Cana. The only difference in Capernaum is the Sea of Galilee and the fishing trade. I want to go to the big cities. I want to experience all the sights and sounds and different nationalities and the food."

...

The boys found the flock grazing on the side of the hill just as Yosef had said.

Eliah said, "Let's go count them. You take that half to the left, and I will take this half to the right."

Azan started counting. Most of the sheep were laying down,

which made it much easier. Eliah met up with him in the middle.

"I count twenty-six. What did *you* get?

"I counted twenty-three. One is missing."

"We better find it. I hope we don't have any predators around. Let's keep our eyes open."

Azan and Eliah went searching around the outer edge of the sheep. As they came to a wooded area, they heard a faint bleating in the bushes on the side of the hill near a small stream. Walking toward the stream, Eliah said, "There it is. Oh, look there's a lamb."

The ewe was lying next to it. As the boys approached her, she got up to her feet and stood in front of the lamb to protect it. Eliah slowly walked toward her. "It is okay, I am not going to hurt your baby." He walked around her and slowly picked up the lamb and carried it back to the large sycamore tree at the bottom of the hill next to the road. The mother followed close behind.

Eliah gently set the lamb down and the ewe came over to it and was nudging it with her nose. "It looks like we have another female." The lamb was unsteady on its feet and struggled to walk. Azan helped guide it until it was next to the ewe. Then it began nursing.

They spent the rest of the afternoon watching out for any predators. The flock was more vulnerable after the birth of a lamb.

Eliah put a rock into his sling and pulled back on the leather strap and let it go. He just barely missed hitting the rock he placed on a tree stump.

Azan laughed and said, "You almost had it."

"We'll see if you can do any better."

He reached down and picked up a small rock, put in his sling, pulled it back, aimed, and let it go. It hit the rock, and it went flying. "How's that for you? I believe I have beat you five out of eight times."

"It was just pure luck—that's all."

They were sitting in the shade as the sun began to sink low in the sky when Yosef and Medad came looking for them. Yosef called to them, "Round up the sheep, and let's head home."

Medad said, "Oh, we have a new lamb?"

Eliah said, "Yes, we found one of the sheep missing when we got here and went looking. The ewe was in the wooded area over there by the stream, and the lamb was lying next to her."

Medad said, "I'm glad you found them before a predator did."

Eliah replied, "It's a female, and she's been nursing just fine."

Medab picked it up and carried it, while its mother anxiously ran alongside with a watchful eye on her lamb.

Eliah asked, "Father, may I come with you to Beth Shan tomorrow? Azan is going, and I would like to come too."

Medad said, "I guess so. Would Heba be willing to feed the sheep in the pen while we're gone? I'll supply some feed for them."

Yosef said, "I don't think she'll mind. The younger boys like to help feed them."

Azan ran ahead to open the gate to the sheep pen, and they ushered all the sheep inside one by one. Medad placed the lamb inside with its mother and closed the gate. They had made the sides of the pen taller than normal and reinforced it to prevent any intruders who could do harm to the sheep during the night. Medad looked around the pen to make sure it was still intact, to be sure the lamb would be safe. Then they said good night and went their separate ways.

"Don't forget to bring your sling tomorrow."

"I won't forget" replied Azan.

When they arrived home, Dobah, Todros, and Meir were playing outside in the courtyard. Dobah had them sitting in front of her, and she was pretending to teach them. She asked Todros to spell his name.

He said, "T-o-d-r-o-s."

Then she turned to Meir asked him to say his numbers.

"One, two, three, four, five."

"That was very good!"

They liked to play school with her. Azan had spent time with Dobah teaching her to read and write, since only boys were allowed in school. His father wasn't very agreeable to it, but he allowed it.

He watched for a moment and then went inside and set his bag down.

Mother was preparing the meal, and Meir came running in, ran to her, grabbed her by the leg, and hugged her.

"Careful, Meir, I have hot food in my hands. Azan, call Dobah and Todros to come in."

They all came to the table and sat down.

After the prayer, Heba asked, "Yosef, when will you be leaving tomorrow for Beth Shan?"

"In the early morning as soon as we can pack and load the donkey. I want to get an early start so we can be there before dark."

"Can you feed the sheep tomorrow? Medab, Eliah, and Azan are coming with me. We'll only be gone over night. It will be a quick trip."

"Yes, I can do that. I'll have Meir help." He looked up at her and smiled from his perch on the bench next to her.

"I prepared food for your journey. I will pack it for you in the morning."

Azan said, "We have a new lamb—it's a female. We found it next to the ewe, by the stream in the wooded area on the side of the hill.

Meir said, "Can I see it?"

Yosef replied, "It's getting dark. You can see it in the morning."

When they had finished their meal, Yosef read from the Scrolls to the family.

Then Azan got up and went to pack for the trip. *I don't think I'll need an extra tunic; I'll take only one cloak. That should be enough for an overnight trip. I will roll up my mat and blanket in the morning. I'll put my sling into my bag now, so I don't forget it.*

He laid awake. *I can only imagine the man from the wilderness who was baptizing people, dressed in camel hair. If he lives in the wilderness, he must have long hair and beard. I wonder what he eats out there. I hope I can find out more about him.*

Life was very predictable, and news like this grabbed his attention.

I am glad Eliah is coming with us tomorrow it will be more fun. I can't wait to see Beth Shan. The trip to the Holy land will be even more remarkable.

Dobah was still awake and asked him, "What are you thinking about?"

"I was just thinking about the things that happened today and the trip tomorrow. That's all. I saw you teaching Meir and Todros today. You are teaching them well. I will make more time for you so you can learn more."

"I would like that. I want to be smart like you."

"Let's get to sleep. I need to get up early tomorrow. Good night, Dobah."

"Good night."

CHAPTER 3

"**A**zan, it's time to get up and be ready to leave. I have your meal ready on the table."
He finished eating and went to gather his mat and blanket.

Outside, Heba handed Yosef the food, and he took it and tied the bag onto the donkey. Medad and Eliah walked up and handed the supplies they brought to Yosef.

Meir came running outside jumping up and down. "Can I come too? I want to go!"

Heba took his hand and said, "Meir, I need you to stay and help me feed the sheep and check on the new lamb."

He loved to be around the new lambs and started jumping again, "Now? Can we go now?"

Heba laughed and said, "Have a good trip," as she started toward the sheep pen with Meir in tow, Dobah and Todros following close behind.

They finished loading the donkey with the food Heba and Galia, Eliah's mother, had prepared. Along with their pads, blankets, extra clothing, and skin bottles filled with water, they added grain for the donkey. They set out towards Beth Shan.

The boys were eager and excited and ran ahead, laughing

and climbing up and down on the rocks. They soon settled into a steady pace with their fathers.

Yosef said, "God has blessed us with a good crop, and we will be able to produce a good batch of wine. With the lambs we sell and the revenue from the wine, we should have enough funding for the winter months."

The boys' energy waned, and they became eager to get to their destination. Azan took his head covering off and wiped the sweat from his face and the back of his neck and asked, "Father, can we stop for a while and have a drink of water?"

"Yes, there's a tree up ahead. We can sit there for a while in the shade."

Medab tied the donkey to the tree and took one of the water skins and passed it to Azan. They all sat down in the cool of the shade.

"Anyone want a piece of bread or fruit?" Eliah asked. He got up and untied the bag of food from the donkey.

Azan spoke up. "I'd like a piece of bread. What fruit do we have?"

"I think we have some figs, dates, and apples."

"I'll take an apple—I can eat it on the way."

"That sounds good, I think I will have one too."

"Father, Medab, do you want a piece of bread or fruit? I think there's dried fish also."

"Yes, I'll take a piece of bread and a piece of dried fish."

"Father, what would you like?"

"I will have the same as Medad."

"Azan, give the donkey some water. The pan is hanging on the other side of him. Only fill it halfway in case he doesn't drink it all. We can't afford to waste any."

After Azan watered the donkey, Eliah took his sling out and picked up a rock. "Hey, Azan, watch this." He put the rock in the sling and pulled back and let go. The rock hit a big knot on a nearby tree and fell to the ground. "I bet you can't do that!"

Azan reached into his bag, which was still attached to the

donkey, and took his sling out. "Watch this!" He found a suitable sized rock and put it in the sling. He pulled it back and let it go and it hit right below the knot.

"Better luck next time," Eliah said.

After they had rested for a half hour, Yosef said, "Let's be on our way. I want to get to the Jewish quarter before dusk."

They approached Beth Shan as the sun was setting low in the sky.

"You were right, Eliah! Look at all the green crops, the fruit trees, and the date palms. And look at the temples. I've never seen any that big."

"I know. I told you."

They came into the town and walked through the marketplace with shops on both sides of the street. It was a wealthy Greek center with a lot of people and activity.

"Eliah, do you smell that? It smells *so* good."

"That's the spice row. It does smell good. I can smell the cinnamon."

"There are spices from all over—more than in our marketplace."

As they walked down the street, the merchants began calling out to them for a purchase. Azan pointed, "Look. Blankets and pottery. There's the fabric for Mother. Do you smell that? The food smells so good, it's making me hungry!

"Look at all the different kinds of olives. What are they cooking in that big pot? Let's see what it is."

"Vegetable stew with lentils. I can smell the garlic and onions in it."

Yosef said, "Come on, the sun is going down, and I want to find a place to stay for the night. We'll eat when we get there."

They made their way to the Jewish quarter on the outskirts of town just as the sun was setting.

There was a row of lean-tos along the roadway for travelers to sleep in overnight; wood framed structures with palm leaf covered tops. They found one that was large enough for all four of them and laid out their mats side by side. There was a communal well in the middle of the quarter, where they refilled the water skins and watered the donkey. The well-worn road had small, humble dwellings on both sides of the street.

People were settling into their homes after a long day. A group of men coming in from their labors walked by and greeted them. "Shalom, how far have you come?"

Standing by the donkey, Medad said, "Shalom, we're here from Cana. Just staying the night."

"Welcome, and we wish you a good night's rest."

"Thank you, to you as well."

Azan marveled at the view. "Look at how the city spreads across the valley and all the lights twinkling." *I never thought to go to the top of the hill over Cana to see the lights of the town. But I don't think it would be as beautiful as this. Beth Shan is larger and more spread out.*

Eliah said, "I'm hungry after smelling all that food in the marketplace. Does anyone want something to eat?"

"What do we have?" Azan asked.

Medab finished securing the donkey to the structure with a rope long enough for it to graze on the vegetation and set out a bucket of grain and more water for him. Then he untied the bag that had their food supplies and brought it over and sat down with the others.

Looking into the bag, he said, "Here, we have sweet bread with dates and dried figs in it and more fruit. Dried fish and barley bread. Let's pray before we eat."

Azan spoke up and said, "God, thank you for the safe journey here today. Thank you for the food you have provided, and we ask that you bless it and those who prepared it."

Then he took a loaf of barley bread, broke it, and passed it around.

Eliah got up and went over to the donkey and untied one of the water skins and took a drink. "Oh, this is so fresh and cold out of the well." And passed it to Azan.

After they had eaten, Yosef quoted scripture. *'The Lord will not allow the righteous to hunger, but He will reject the craving of the wicked. Poor is he who works with a negligent hand, but the hand of the diligent makes rich. He who gathers in summer is a son who acts wisely, but he who sleeps in harvest is a son who acts shamefully. Blessings are on the head of the righteous, but the mouth of the wicked conceals violence. The memory of the righteous is blessed, but the name of the wicked will rot. The wise in heart will receive commands, but a babbling fool will be ruined. He who walks in integrity walks securely, but he who perverts his ways will be found out.'*

Medab added, "It would be best for you two to heed these sayings."

Azan replied, "I want to follow God's commands, and walk in integrity. You and father have been good examples of this. You both work hard to support your families, and you strive to keep God's commands."

Azan laid down and looked up at the heavens and prayed to himself. *Father God, please give me wisdom to walk in integrity and follow your commands. I want to please you in all my ways. Amen.*

It had been a long day. It was dark, and they soon fell asleep.

∾

They got up early and went to the marketplace. The familiar aromas were again tickling Azan's senses. They found the spice row and sought out the items that Galia had asked for.

Azan walked up to one of the booths and said, "Here's the cinnamon."

Eliah pointed. "There's the curry, turmeric, and Syrian hyssop."

The merchant started encouraging a sale by calling out to Medad, who was looking at what the boys had pointed out.

The streets were bustling with activity and chatter. While the men negotiated with the merchant, Azan was looking around, and he heard a group of people talking. One of the men said, "There's a man baptizing people in the Jordan River."

Azan looked at Eliah, and they moved a little closer so they could hear them.

The other man said, "I was there, and I was astonished at his wisdom. He was a young man in his thirties. He must be a prophet. The prophets have been silent for the last four hundred years. He baptizes people only after they have repented of their sins. He says the long-awaited kingdom of heaven is near."

Azan looked at Eliah with surprise. Then the man said, "Multitudes of people were coming to him to be baptized."

Another man who overheard their conversation spoke up and said, "That man is nothing more than a false prophet. Don't listen to him."

The first man said, "You don't know that. I think this may be the beginning of a turn of events."

The other man said, "You don't know anything."

"If you had heard him, you might think differently."

The other man huffed and walked away.

Azan turned to Eliah and said, "I have never heard of anything like that before. Who *is* this man?"

"I don't know. He *could* be a new prophet."

Azan noticed that Medad had completed his purchase.

Yosef called to them, "Come on, let's move on."

They continued walking, and Azan pointed, "There's the fabric."

Yosef looked through the ribbon and selected the purple color Heba had asked for. He looked at the fabric and said, "There are too many shades of purple. I will have to guess which one she wanted. I'll take the whole length of this fabric." He handed it to the merchant.

Eliah was looking around and said, "Father, the grains are over here."

Medad paid the merchant for barley, and they added it to the donkey's load.

Yosef asked the boys, "Do you want to purchase something to eat before we begin our journey?"

Eliah looked around at the booths and saw something he wanted. "Can we have the figs stuffed with honey and almonds? They have them right over there."

Azan added, "Can we get some kuddah bread? We can put the figs into the pocket."

Yosef laughed. "You two sure like the sweet tastes. Get what you want." The sun is rising in the sky. We must be on our way back to Cana. Place the food in the bag, and we'll have it later. Take an apple for now and eat it on the way."

They walked quietly along for a period. Azan spoke up. "We heard a man in the marketplace say that the one they call the Baptist might be a prophet. Another man said he is nothing but a false prophet. The first man said he thinks it's the beginning of a turn of events. He said multitudes of people are coming to him to be baptized, and that the long-awaited kingdom of heaven was near."

Medad said, "More and more people are listening to him preach and believing his words. I heard that the Baptist pointed to a man and said, 'Behold! The Lamb of God who takes away the sin of the world!'"

The boys looked at each other in wonder.

Azan thought, *could this be the beginning of the coming kingdom? What does he mean, the Lamb of God who takes away the sin of the world?*

Azan asked, "What does he mean by the Lamb of God?"

Eliah replied, "Remember our teacher told us that we should be looking forward to the Kingdom of God? Could this be the Messiah?"

Azan's eyes grew big, and he hoped it was true. Eliah laughed at him. "I'm just kidding you. I don't think he is the Messiah. I got you with that one!"

Yosef said, "That's enough. Let's not get all caught up in this. We need to follow what we know from scripture. It is God's word—we should only listen to Him."

After stopping two times to rest in the shade and walking for hours, they arrived home. Medad and Eliah gathered their things and went on their way.

Heba greeted them at the door. "How was the trip?" Yosef said, "It went well. Here are the things you asked for."

She looked through the fabric and said, "This color is perfect. The ribbon is just the right color also. Thank you."

Exhausted from the long trip, Azan went and laid down on his bed right after the meal and his father's reading of scripture.

I wonder who the Baptist is. I wonder if he is a prophet.

Could this mean that the Messiah is coming? I hope he is.

God, only you know when your Messiah will come. Please help me to know if he comes, that it is truly him. Amen.

CHAPTER 4

Azan's mother worked the next couple of weeks with the other women, preparing for the wedding in Cana. The daughter of her close friend was getting married, and the women in the community came together to help with the decorations and the food that could be prepared in advance.

∾

The long-awaited wedding feast had arrived. The trumpet sounded, and all the people in Cana started gathering to celebrate.

Azan met up with Eliah and said, "Are you ready for a fun week? Don't you love it when there's a wedding in town? I love all the different kinds of food like roast chicken, rice, lamb, vegetables and all the different breads and fruit."

Eliah added, "I love the apple cakes and the pears in spice sauce. And I like listening to the rhythmic music and watching the lively dancing."

Heba came and found the boys and said, "We could use

your help in moving the tables into place. Put them in rows of three and place the benches, which are over there, around each one for the people to sit on." They were happy to help. Azan grabbed the end of a table and Eliah the other end. Azan pulled one way, and Eliah pulled the other way and scolded him, "Move it this way!"

"Okay! I thought you were going that way!" he said in a sarcastic tone.

They placed the two-and-a-half-foot-high long tables into place and put four benches on each side, with one at each end. The women gathered the decorations and began placing them in the center of each of the purple cloth-covered tables.

The festivities began, and the people started filtering in. One of the women who was helping looked up and got excited when she saw a young man and his friends come through the entrance. She ran over and hugged him and welcomed them. The mother of the bride went and invited them to sit and eat. People came in and greeted the bride, the groom, and their parents. Then they found a place to sit and started eating and drinking. The boys watched as the servants poured the wine and kept the tables full of food. They found a place and filled their plates.

"What did you get? I'm having lamb, bread, olives, and figs."

Eliah replied, "I'm having chicken, bread, and rice. I'll have olives. Please pass them to me."

Azan looked around and thought, *The decorations make the place look festive. The purple cloth on the tables that Mother brought looks beautiful. The lit candles in the center of the tables with the flowers and greenery encircling them really add to it.* He looked around at the walls and thought, *the flowers tied with the purple ribbon around them make this everyday place look special and festive.*

He said, "The women did a great job. The place looks nice."

"Yes, it does look nice. It makes the ordinary look extraordinary."

The wedding feast continued into the second and third day, with the people eating, drinking, dancing, and laughing. The servants kept food on the tables and wine in their cups.

On the fourth day, the boys were sitting at a table, again sampling the food.

Azan said, "I do not think I can eat another bite. Want to walk around?"

Eliah grabbed another piece of apple cake and got up. They started walking and came to the place where the stone waterpots sat. They saw the same woman who had greeted a man and his friends' days earlier, talking to him again. They heard her say to him, "There's no more wine. They have run out!"

He replied, **"Woman, what does that have to do with me? My hour has not yet come."**

She said, "If not now, when?"

She turned to the servants and said, "Whatever He says to you, do it" and she walked away.

The man looked up and closed his eyes as if he were praying. Then he told the servants, **"Fill the waterpots with water."**

The two boys watched as the servants filled them to the brim. Then the man said to one of the servants, **"Draw some out now, and take it to the headwaiter."**

The servant dipped a stone cup into one of the pots and filled it to the top. The servant looked at the cup and smelled it. He got a shocked look on his face, turned, and looked at the man. Then he went to find the headwaiter.

Azan said, "Let's follow him."

They followed closely behind the servant until he found the headwaiter. He handed it to him to taste. He took a sip, and he looked surprised.

He called the bridegroom aside and said to him, "Every man

serves the good wine first, and when the people have drunk freely, then he serves the poorer wine; but you have kept the good wine until now."

The groom looked equally surprised, as he tasted it. His eyes grew big, and he told the servant, "Go and serve the guests." He took his bride to the center of the room and instructed the musicians to play. They encouraged everyone to get up and dance.

Eliah looked at Azan, "We watched them put water in those waterpots! It was water, wasn't it?"

Azan looked at the headwaiter and then to Eliah. "It couldn't be wine. We were there and watched the servants pour water into the waterpots, and now it's wine? Who *is* that man, and how could he turn water into wine? I've never seen anything like that before."

"That is unbelievable—how did he do that? Let's go back and look in those waterpots."

They ran back to the waterpots, and they saw the servants standing around them in amazement at what they had witnessed.

Azan went to the waterpots and investigated each one and said, "They are all filled with wine. Every one of them!"

Eliah investigated each one and looked at the servants. They looked just as astonished as he was, as they filled the pitchers.

"Who would ever believe what just happened? I bet if we told anyone, they would think we made it up." Azan said.

"I'm sure they would make fun of us. I'm not going to mention it to anyone."

Azan said, "Let's find that man. Let's see where he went."

They found him sitting with his friends. They sat at a table near them and watched them get up and take part in the dancing and then they sat around the table talking and laughing.

The same woman came over to him and cupped his face in

her hands, kissed his cheek, and thanked him. They were close enough to hear her say, "The parents and the wedding couple were very pleased and thankful for not running out of wine, which would have been shameful." She smiled at him and walked away.

The feast went on for the entire week, and the boys indulged themselves with lamb, chicken, the different breads, fruit, cooked grains, olives, dates, figs, grapes, apple cakes, and the spiced pears. Weddings were rare in Cana, and they didn't want it to end. It was an eventful week that the boys would not soon forget.

∞

Over the next few weeks, Azan heard people talking about a man who was teaching and healing people with his hands. He heard stories of his remarkable powers, and the news was spreading from town to town.

At home one night, the family was sitting around the table for their meal. Heba asked Yosef, "There is talk in town about a new teacher, a miracle worker. Have you heard of him? Do you know who he is?"

Yosef said, "I don't know who he is, but people are saying that they have seen him curing the blind, the lame, and the sick by the power of his voice and the mere touch of his hands. I've heard that people are impressed by his teachings and signs. I don't know about this—he could be a false teacher. We must be extremely cautious and not be deceived by any false teachings. The Pharisees are getting concerned about him. They think he could influence people to go away from our laws and traditions."

Azan had never heard of anything like this before. *I want to know more about this man. I really want to hear him speak. Could he be the long-awaited Messiah?* A month had passed since the wedding and the trip to the Passover was coming up in a little over a week. Heba had worked baking bread and making food for the trip to take with them.

She arranged clothing and supplies for the three younger children. Azan's grandparents lived with Heba's sister Shalva and her family on the other side of Cana. On occasion, they would come to stay at the house with the children when Yosef and Heba were away.

2

The day arrived, and Heba gave last-minute instructions to her parents. "Meir should be in bed shortly after sundown. The other two can stay up for a while longer. I have food prepared for all of you to make it easier on you."

Yosef packed their food and supplies and strapped them to their donkey.

Azan had just celebrated his twelfth birthday and asked his father, "Who will be celebrating my Bar Mitzvah with us in the Holy City?"

"My sister Ahava and Reuben. They have moved to the lower city in Jerusalem. They will be there together with Eliah's family and us. We promised them we would celebrate in the Holy City so they could take part. Are you prepared for your big day?"

"Yes, I have been studying for the last two years for this. I have finished writing my speech. I'm excited and a little nervous. I haven't spoken in front of people before, only in school."

"You'll do good. It will be a joy for your mother and I to present you."

They met Eliah and his family at the town center and began their journey.

The roads became crowded with hundreds of pilgrims making the trip to Jerusalem.

Azan picked up a stick that was as tall as him to use as a staff. "Eliah, find a stick for your staff."

Eliah looked around and found one that was shorter than him. He picked it up and started walking with it next to Azan.

After a couple of hours, they got tired of that. Eliah dropped his staff and picked up a rock and threw it at an outcropping of rocks on the side of the road.

Azan said, "I bet I can hit that rock over by that tree." It was farther than the outcropping. He picked up a rock, took a step forward, and threw the rock, hitting right in front of the target.

Yosef scolded them, "You two be careful, there are a lot of people around."

They continued as they walked along to see who could throw a rock the farthest, being careful not to throw in the direction of any people.

"Let's stop and rest in the shade for a while. You boys, water the donkey." They looked for a tree that had room under it. There were so many people, it was hard to find one that had shade available.

At sunset, they arrived in Beth Shan with the other caravans. They made their way to the Jewish quarter, where they had spent the night on their earlier trip.

The travel structures were all taken along the roadway where they had stayed before. They found a family that was willing to house them overnight for a small fee. With the women along, they preferred to have an enclosed shelter.

Eliah said to Azan, "Let's sleep outside so we can see the stars."

They went outside, and Azan pointed to a place next to the house. "How about right here?"

"Sure, this looks okay."

"I am tired after all that walking. We still have three more days before we get there."

"I know. Tomorrow will be another long day, but it will be worth it."

They unrolled their mats and laid down.

Azan looked at all the city lights in the valley. "Beth Shan seems small when you're in the town, but it looks large from up here."

They both laid there looking up into the heavens, grew quiet, and fell asleep.

CHAPTER 5

O n day two, they woke up, ate, and started on their
way. They chose to go through Samaria to lessen
the travel time. The road was a level, straight road
that was easy to travel, just as Eliah had described. There were
no towns for miles, only the stone fortresses staffed by military
soldiers who stood watch over the pilgrims as they passed.

"Azan, it's your turn to take the donkey. Here take him for a
while."

"Okay."

The sun was directly over them, and he walked over and
took the reins. As he took his head covering off and wiped his
brow, he stumbled on a rock and the donkey jerked back and
stopped. Azan tugged on the rope to get him to move, but he
just stood there.

Azan complained. "Come on, stubborn old mule" and
pulled on the rope with more force. With Azan's insistence, he
finally obliged.

"Are you going to let that beast get the better of you?"

"No, he knows who's boss."

Eliah laughed at him.

"What are you laughing at? He moved, didn't he?"

Heba said, "Now boys, let's be nice to each other." They continued all day, taking short breaks to rest and to get out of the sun.

As they approached Sukkoth, Yosef said, "We will stop here. We will not be welcome in Sukkoth. The Samaritans do not want the Jews in their towns. It would be best if we stay near this military post overnight. It will be safer."

Azan saw the town a mile or so in the distance. They gathered around the people in the other Caravans for more protection.

The third day was just as long, until Eliah said, "Look we are coming up to Bethel. The last stop before Jerusalem."

Azan could see the heat rising from the ground in the distance, and it made the town look wavy.

Yosef said, "Secure the donkey and unload what we need for the night."

After the meal, the men gathered to pray. Azan and Eliah joined them and listened to the men talk about the scrolls.

They laid down, staring up at the darkening sky as the stars slowly appeared one by one. Just then a shooting star streaked across the sky.

"Did you see that?" Azan asked.

"Yes, that one went far!"

"I heard that thousands of people go to Jerusalem each year."

"It was very crowded last year. You must push your way through the streets. There are people from all over, all nationalities and different languages."

"I can hardly wait to see it all."

Azan rolled over on his mat and closed his eyes.

∞

It was the fourth day of their journey. They gathered up their belongings and continued to walk along the roadway, making sure they stayed in the outskirts of Sukkoth to avoid any confrontation. It was as uneventful as the day before. Finally, they climbed the ridge that rose from the desert floor toward Jerusalem.

"I'm excited that we're almost there!"

Eliah replied, "Just wait until you see it. The Holy City is amazing."

They could see glimpses of it off in the distance. The gray desert turned into cultivated fields of green, and there were vineyards, rows of olive trees, fruit trees, date palms, and homes that dotted the land.

As they reached the ridge, they could see the city and the buildings that were grander than in Beth Shan.

Then Azan saw it. "Look, there's the temple. It's majestic! Look at the white and gold walls! There are the courts! There are so many people, look at all of them."

Eliah chimed in, "Do you see the Roman soldiers? They stand guard to keep control of the crowds. You don't want to mess with them. It will not go well for you if you cross paths with one of them. They have no problem putting people in prison for little or no reason."

Azan was amazed at all he was seeing. They followed the pilgrims through the Golden Gate into the crowded city.

There were tens of thousands of people from all over. Azan heard people talking in different languages and saw some in colorful clothing, and they smelled of incense as they passed by. There were people from Galilee, Judea, Babylonia, and parts of the Roman Empire.

Heba placed her hand on his shoulder and told him, "Stay close so we don't get separated."

There was so much activity, noise, and things to look at, Azan could hardly take in all in.

Yosef asked a man in a booth, "Can you direct us to a place where we can stay while in town?"

"I can direct you to a place, which is available, but you must stay for at least five nights. There is a modest charge, but there is ample room for all six of you.

Medad said, "I will share the cost with you," and they paid the man.

He said, "Follow me."

Once at the house, he directed the men to a place where they could stable the donkey.

Heba said, "Galia and I will go buy food and supplies from the marketplace. We'll get what is needed for

Passover and for Azan's Bar Mitzvah."

The women left, and the men unloaded the donkey and brought things inside.

Yosef took the donkey to stable him and paid the man for his keep.

∾

The next day the boys joined their fathers and went to the temple to buy a lamb from the merchants. The men picked a year-old lamb without blemish and paid for it.

Medad told Yosef, "It should be a crime for charging so much for the lambs. They're taking advantage of the pilgrims."

Yosef explained, "This lamb is for a sacrifice to the

Lord, the lifeblood of the animal belongs to the Lord." Medad placed the lamb on his shoulders, and they made their way through the courtyard of the temple.

There were people everywhere, vendors and money changers, animals, and the Roman soldiers. They walked through the crowds toward the Court of Israel, where only the male Jews could enter.

They entered the court, and Azan saw the magnificent stone altar surrounded by the white marble and gold walls of the sanctuary. As they waited for the sacrifices to begin, more people pushed in around them with their lambs, rams, and doves. There were so many people that they did the sacrifices from morning till late afternoon.

Then the trumpet sounded, and Eliah pointed to the High Priest, who began the procession. He was wearing a white linen robe, a coat embroidered with purple and scarlet, a breastplate with twelve precious stones, and a turban with a crown on his head, which had "Holy to the Lord" written on it.

Behind him came the other priests, with still others playing Lyres and singing, *"Give thanks to the Lord, for he is good, his lovingkindness is everlasting!"* They took their places in front of the altar and began to offer the sacrifices.

When it was their turn, Yosef handed the lamb over to the priests, and they took it, slaughtered it, skinned, and dressed it. They sprinkled the blood on the horns of the altar.

Azan and Eliah watched intensely as the priests took the fat and burned it on the fire. Then they wrapped a part of the lamb in a cloth and handed it back to Yosef.

They started to walk out through the temple when they heard someone yelling. Azan looked through the crowd and saw a man with his back turned to him. He was swinging a whip and yelling at the vendors telling them, *"Take these things away"*

Azan was close enough to see the man turning over tables with the money thrown to the ground. The man told the vendors selling the sheep, oxen, and doves, **"Stop making My Father's house a place of business."**

Then he said to them, *'It is written, My Father's house will be called a house of prayer, but you are making it a robber's den.'*

People started scattering away. Azan was watching the man when he turned toward him, and he realized that it was the same man that turned the water into wine at the wedding in Cana. Azan looked at Eliah with wide-open eyes, and they were both amazed. Then people brought forward a man that was lame. Azan watched as the man from the wedding placed his hands on the lame man and said something, but he couldn't hear his words. The lame man got up and was laughing and jumping up and down. Then the crowd brought a blind man to him, and he healed him with his words. The people began crying out in the temple, *"Hosanna to the Son of David!"*

Azan looked at all the people witnessing this and saw the chief priests and the scribes talking about what they were seeing, and they asked the teacher, "Do you hear what they are saying?"

The man said, "Yes; have you never read, ***'Out of the mouth of infants and nursing babies you have prepared praise for yourself'?'"*** And he went out of the temple and disappeared into the crowd.

Medad ushered the boys out of the temple court, and they walked back to where they were staying.

On the way Azan said, "Who is that man? How is he able to heal people?"

Yosef replied, "I don't know. Only God can heal. He may be planning these things to gain a following. He could be demon possessed. We just don't know. I'll say it again, we can't allow ourselves to be deceived."

CHAPTER 6

T he next day was the day of preparation, and the women were busy preparing the food for the Passover meal. They made unleavened bread, a fruit and nut paste, and raw vegetables dipped in tart dressing. They had secured enough wine and arranged the room with floor cushions around the table. They gathered in the evening and rested after their long trip.

∾

The day of Passover had arrived, and everything was prepared. The men spent the day slow roasting the lamb over a fire and had it ready by the evening.

When the food was ready, they sat down to eat, and Yosef gave the Passover blessing.

He began, 'We need to be reminded of all that the Passover celebration is and to remember that God delivered Israel out of the hands of the Egyptians. *"Moses called for all the elders of Israel and said to them, 'Go and take for yourselves lambs according to your families and slay the Passover lamb.*

You shall take a bunch of hyssops and dip it in the blood, which is in the basin, and apply some of the blood that is in the basin to the lintel and the two doorposts; and none of you shall go outside the door of his house until morning. For the Lord will pass through to smite the Egyptians; and when He sees the blood on the lintel and on the two doorposts, the Lord will pass over the door and will not allow the destroyer to come into your houses to smite you. And you shall observe this event as an ordinance for you and your children forever.'"

Then he prayed for deliverance from the ongoing oppression of the Roman Empire. They sat and ate and relaxed at the table, enjoying the feast and conversation.

Yosef asked Azan, "What does the Passover lamb remind us of?"

"It reminds us of the faith of our ancestors."

"Yes, that's right."

"Eliah, what is the significance of the bitter herbs?"

"It reminds us of the bitterness of their slavery."

"That's correct."

"Medad, what about the unleavened bread?"

"It represents their hasty departure from Egypt."

"Galia, tell me why we have the nut-and-fruit paste."

"It helps us to remember the clay they made into bricks for Pharoah."

"Heba, what do the cups of wine represent?"

"It reminds us of God's promises to his people."

"Therefore, we celebrate the Passover each year, that we do not forget all that God has done."

∞

After dinner, Yosef, Medad, Azan, and Eliah sat outside.
Azan spoke up and said, "The man in the temple, he was at

the wedding in Cana, and Eliah and I were next to the waterpots and saw that same man ask the servants to fill the waterpots with water. Then the man told the servants to draw some out of one of the waterpots. He told him to take it to the headwaiter.

"We were curious, so we followed the servant. The headwaiter tasted it and pulled the bridegroom aside and said that usually the best wine is served first, but you have saved the best wine until now."

Medad said, "I heard about that, but I didn't believe it. But you say you two saw it happen?"

Eliah said, "Yes, we saw it all! We said nothing because we didn't think anyone would believe us. We even went back to the waterpots and looked in each one, and they were all filled with wine."

Medad asked, "Are you sure he was the same man? He was pretty upset with the merchants! He certainly didn't want them selling inside the temple."

Azan asked, "Yes, I recognized him. Did you see how he was healing the blind and lame people? How is he able to do that?"

Medad said, "We have heard that a man has been going around healing people and preaching in the Synagogues. This must be the same man."

Yosef said, "Enough of this. We do not know who this man is. Only God can heal."

Azan couldn't help himself and said, "What if he's the one we've been waiting for?"

His father looked at him in a stern way and he knew he had overstepped his boundary.

They sat and talked for the rest of the night, while the women cleaned up and rested inside. The boys listened to Yosef's teachings concerning the temple and what the Scrolls says about the sacrifices and why they are necessary.

Azan had a tough time going to sleep that night. *I will celebrate my Bar Mitzvah tomorrow. I will be recognized as a member of the Jewish community. I'll have to be responsible for my actions and for knowing the law and our Jewish traditions. I will be able to lead prayer services and read from the Scrolls to the family and the community. I have spent years studying for this very moment.*

CHAPTER 7

Morning came, and they sat around eating breakfast and talking about the day's festivities. Smiling, Azan said, "Today I celebrate my Bar Mitzvah."

Heba said, "I can see you're excited. It *is* a milestone."

After they ate, he sat on his bed and studied his speech to make sure he was ready. He put on his best clothes, and Yosef placed his yarmulkes on his head.

Yosef looked at him with teary eyes and said, "Today, you are coming of age. I am proud of you."

Azan hugged Yosef and said, "I will make you proud, follow all the traditions and keep my responsibilities."

∞

Heba and Eliah's family followed Azan and Yosef as they made their way to the Synagogue. As they entered, Azan took a deep breath. He saw Ahava, his aunt, and her husband, Tobias, sitting inside with many others.

"Thank you for coming. It's good to see you both."

Yosef went before the congregation and said, "Azan, will you come stand here beside me? Heba, please join us. Today our son Azan is of age. His mother and I hereby present him to the Jewish community. Azan, do you have something to say?"

His heart raced. He cleared his throat and said, "Thank you for being here with me on this special day. It is important to me that you are all witnesses today as I affirm my Jewish identity. I am now responsible for positive acts of kindness to those less fortunate than myself. This creates a link between God and humanity.

"As I become a Bar Mitzvah, I will read from the Torah in public for the first time." Then he read a section of the Torah from the scroll.

Yosef said a special blessing over Azan. "God, I thank you for my son on this day, and I declare him a member of the Jewish community."

Azan looked at his parents with love in his eyes and said, "Thank you, Father. Thank you, Mother."

Eliah and his family came and gathered around and congratulated him on his new status.

Ahava and Tobias walked over to him, and she hugged him. "We are proud of you. Congratulations, Azan."

They all went back to the house and held a party to celebrate. Yosef and Heba came to Azan. Yosef said, "Son, we would like to present you with this gift. This book has been in our family for years and passed down from generation to generation. It is a family book concerning our Jewish faith and culture."

"Thank you, I am honored to receive it."

Eliah said, "Azan, come sit next to me."

He sat down and filled his plate, and they ate until Tobias picked up his twelve stringed Nevel and began to play. Yosef took Heba by the hand and they began to dance around the room. They walked over to Azan and grabbed his arm and pulled him into the rhythmic dancing. Then Medad and Galia and Eliah joined in with Ahava, while Tobias kept playing. He was happy to see how joyful his parents were.

The party went on late into the night, and everyone ate, drank, danced, and enjoyed each other.

Passover week continued through the next day. Azan and Eliah were given freedom to roam around the city. They went to the marketplace to see all the wares and admire all the different sights and aromas.

They stopped to watch a demonstration on how to cook with certain spices when Azan heard the man next to them tell another, "John the Baptist has been arrested."

Azan turned to the man and asked, "Why was he arrested"?

The man said, "John had told Herodias that it was not lawful for him to have his brother's wife. The people are upset about John's arrest."

He went on. "This is what John the Baptist said before he was arrested, '*For He whom God sent speaks the words of God; for He gives the Spirit without measure. The Father loves the son and has given all things into his hands. He who believes in the Son has eternal life, but he who does not obey the Son will not see life, but the wrath of God abides on him.*"

Azan asked, "Was he talking about the Messiah"?

The man replied. "I cannot say that he is or is not talking about the Messiah."

The man turned away and continued to talk to the other man. Eliah and Azan spent the day looking for the man they had seen in the temple. The one who turned water into wine. They both wanted to find out more about him. They were disappointed when they didn't find him.

∾

The family prepared to leave the following day and had packed their belongings when the boys returned from their day of adventure.

They had to leave before the week of celebration was completely over. They needed to start for home.

∾

Yosef said, "Azan, take charge of the donkey."

He grabbed the rope, and they started their journey out of the city. They maneuvered their way through the crowded streets and through the Golden Gate. Azan stopped at the top of the hill, turned, and looked at the city, the temple, and all the people still coming and going. He wanted to remember what it looked like because he knew he would not see it again for a while. His parents were in the habit of journeying to the Passover only every other year.

Azan told Eliah, "I wish we could have seen the teacher before we left. I want to know more about him. I hope we run into him somewhere so we can listen to him."

Azan felt more grown up, more accountable, and didn't want to walk on the rock walls or throw stones.

He reflected on his Bar Mitzvah. "I am included with the men now and I have to live up to my promises." He felt as if a weight had come upon him. "I have to be responsible."

They entered the desert and began their long walk. After an hour, Azan took his head covering off and wiped his face and the back of his neck. *I wonder what will happen to John the Baptist. Was he talking about the Messiah when he said that the one God has sent speaks the word of God?*

The family took breaks under the shade of the trees and then continued past Bethel.

∾

They stopped for the evening meal and to sleep under the stars, again by an outpost for safety. It got dark, and Yosef came over and laid his mat between Heba and Azan.

43

Azan had not had a chance to talk to him about what he heard. "Father, when Eliah and I were in the marketplace, we heard a man next to us say that they had arrested John the Baptist. He said that the people were upset about it."

Yosef replied, "I hadn't heard that. Did he say why they arrested him?"

"The man said the Baptist spoke against Herodias, about him taking his brother's wife. Herodias had him thrown into jail.

"He also said, that before they arrested him, the Baptist made it sound like this man who is going around teaching and healing is the Son of God. Could the man we saw in the temple be the Messiah?"

Yosef replied, "We have been looking for the Messiah to appear for a long time. I do not know if he is the Messiah or not. We have been expecting that the Messiah will come with power, defeat the Roman rule over Israel, and set us free from their oppression. I want you to be careful of what you believe. I know this all interests you, but we must stick with the truth that we have in the scriptures. Let's go to sleep. We have another long day ahead of us."

Azan fell asleep, staring at the stars and thinking about the past week and all that had occurred. The journey continued, and the days were long, hot, and dry.

CHAPTER 8

They went to Nazareth so that Heba could visit her cousin and let the women rest while the men went to the Synagogue.

Azan and Eliah entered with the others and sat down.

Then a man stood up to read. He took a scroll and began reading. He said the reading was from the prophet Isaiah. Azan was looking around the inside of the Synagogue since he had never been inside this one before. When his eyes adjusted to the dimly lit room, he looked at the man standing in front of those gathered.

He nudged Eliah. "Look, it's the teacher!"

They both watched him with wide eyes.

He read: *'The Spirit of the Lord God is upon me, Because the Lord has anointed me to bring good news to the afflicted; He has sent me to bind up the brokenhearted, To proclaim liberty to captives and freedom to prisoners; To proclaim the favorable year of the Lord.'* Then he rolled up the scroll, gave it back to the attendant, and sat down. The eyes of everyone in the synagogue were on him.

And He began by saying to them, "**Today this scripture is fulfilled in your hearing.**"

All spoke well of him and were amazed at the gracious words that came from his lips.

Then one said, "Is this not Joseph's son Jesus?"

Jesus said to them, "**No doubt you will quote this proverb to me: 'Physician, heal yourself! Whatever we heard was done at Capernaum, do here in your hometown as well.'**

"**Truly I say to you,**" he continued. "**No prophet is welcome in his hometown. But I say to you in truth, there were many widows in Israel in the days of Elijah, when the sky was shut for three years and six months, when a famine came over all the land; and yet Elijah was sent to none of them, but only to Zarephath, in the land of Sidon. And there were many lepers in Israel in the time of Elisha the prophet, and none of them was cleansed, but only Naaman the Syrian.**"

All the people in the synagogue became furious when they heard this. They knew he was referring to them.

They got up, drove him out of town, and took him to the top of the hill to throw him off the cliff. Azan followed the others, and when they reached the ridge, the teacher walked right through the crowd and started on his way.

Azan watched him walk away and was devastated by the reaction of these men. He was taught in school about the Messiah that would come, and he hoped to witness it in his lifetime. He wanted to believe that this man *was* the Messiah. His eyes welled up with tears. He could hardly hold his emotions inside.

He was looking at him as he walked away, and then Jesus turned around and looked straight at Azan and smiled briefly at him. Azan felt something that he had never felt before. It was as if Jesus was looking deep within him. Then He just walked away, no one touched him.

Then Yosef grabbed his shoulder and said, "Come away from here." He followed the men back into town. The men were still angry and were complaining among themselves.

On the walk back to where the women were resting, Azan said, "Why did the men get so angry with the teacher?"

Yosef said, "They were angry because he claimed to be from God, but it is known that he is from Nazareth.

He is a man, and he claims to be from God?"

Azan replied, "But what if he *is* from God?"

Yosef scolded him, saying, "You have a lot to learn. Wisdom comes with age. We must follow what we know. We have to follow scripture."

He looked over at Eliah, who raised his finger to his mouth as if to try to hush him.

Azan was disappointed. *Those men have it all wrong about this Jesus. There is something about him that I cannot explain. I have this inner feeling that what Jesus said was true. I know it in my heart. I must find out more about Jesus. I want to know the truth.*

On the way from Nazareth to Cana, Eliah took Azan aside and warned him. "Azan, you are going to get yourself in a lot of trouble if you are not careful. Your father is a leader under the Pharisees. He will not be happy with you if you cross the line with this Jesus. I understand how you feel, but is it worth it to anger your father?"

"I know what you are saying, but what if he is the Messiah and we miss it? Do we want God to be angry with us if Jesus *is* His son and we reject him? I must know if he is the Messiah or not. I must have confirmation one way or the other. This isn't something that I take lightly. I know the gravity of going against my father, or worst, going against God. I will be careful in my pursuit of the truth."

"How will you know the truth?"

"Father says we must follow what scripture says. I will search the scriptures and study the prophesies about the

Messiah. I pray that God will lead me and show me the truth."

I don't want to cause problems for father, but I have a strong sense that Jesus is who he says he is. I must confirm it in my heart and in my mind. God, if I am wrong about Jesus, please let me know.

CHAPTER 9

It was the beginning of the week, and the usual routine unfolded with Azan going to school. Walking to school, he thought, *Father said that we need to follow scripture. And that is what I will do. I want to study Isaiah. The very words that Jesus read in the Synagogue. I want to search and understand them.*

He approached his Rabbi. "I want to read and study the book of Isaiah. If you don't mind, can read it during my free time and after school? There are some passages that I want to understand." His Rabbi was pleased to see his interest and agreed.

Azan began his journey of discovery and spent time reading the book of Isaiah every chance he got. He came to Isaiah 61:1-2 and read it to himself. '***The Spirit of the Lord God is upon me, Because the Lord has anointed me to bring good news to the afflicted; He has sent me to bind up the brokenhearted, To proclaim liberty to the captives and freedom to prisoners; To proclaim the favorable year of the Lord.***'

Is he talking about rescuing people? Setting them free! I want to know about Jesus, the so-called Nazarene. How could he claim to be the Son of God? We studied the scripture that says, 'But you, Bethlehem, Ephratah, though you be little among the clans of Judah, out of you will come for me one who will be ruler over Israel, whose origins are from of old, from ancient times.'

The Messiah would have to come from Ephratah, Bethlehem. But Jesus is from Nazareth, like the men said.

The words Jesus spoke in the Synagogue still lingered in his thoughts. He sensed he was missing something.

∞

In the town square after school one day, his brothers were fighting over a toy that his mother had made for them. As he watched them, a man came through the square saying that Herodias had ordered the beheading of John the Baptist. A group of men took his body away to bury it.

He said, "Jesus, the teacher, went to stay in Capernaum."

Azan was saddened by the news about John the Baptist. *How could they kill him for just telling the truth? It's not lawful to take your brother's wife if he is still living. Jesus went to Capernaum. I wonder how long he will be there. That's not too far from here.*

∞

As time went on, he heard about the teachings of Jesus in and around Galilee. People were amazed that his words had such power and authority. The news was spreading about how Jesus had the power to drive out demons; how they would come out shouting, "You are the Son of God!" and how he healed people of various kinds of sickness by laying his hands on them.

I wish I could be present to see these things. I hope Jesus is the Messiah. But how can he be if he was born in Nazareth, not Bethlehem?

When Jesus was in the Synagogue in Nazareth, he said,

"The Spirit of the Lord is upon me." What did he mean? He read in Isaiah 11:1-2, which says, 'Then a shoot will spring from the stem of Jesse; And a branch from his roots will bear fruit. The Spirit of the Lord shall rest on him, the spirit of wisdom and understanding, the spirit of counsel and strength, the spirit of knowledge and the fear of the Lord.'

I remember what John the Baptist said before he was arrested. 'For he whom God has sent speaks the words of God, for He gives the Spirit without measure. The Father loves the son and has given all things into his hand. He who believes in the Son has eternal life, but he who does not obey the Son will not see life, but the wrath of God abides on him.'

He pondered these things while out watching the sheep. How does all this fit together?

∽

Azan came home after bringing the sheep in. Heba was sitting outside, watching the children, sitting on a bench while sewing.

He sat down next to her and asked, "Mother, do you remember the wedding we went to not long ago?"

"Yes, what about it?"

"Did you hear anything about them running out of wine?"

"Yes, I remember that they were in a panic about it. But they ended up with more wine than they needed."

"A man named Jesus was there, and a woman asked him to help them. I saw the servants fill the waterpots with water. He looked up, closed his eyes, and prayed. Then he told the servants to draw a cup out of the one of the pots and take it to the headwaiter. He tasted it and said that it was better than the wine with which they had started."

She said, "You saw that? I heard about it, but it didn't make any sense to me."

"I saw the same woman walk over to where he was sitting and kissed him and thanked him."

"Mary was one of the women that was helping with the wedding. I saw her go over and kiss the man she had introduced to me as her son. We had talked earlier, and she said her son Jesus had come from a distance to attend the wedding.

"He is the one everyone is talking about. The one who has been performing miracles. He is Jesus, and they are from Nazareth, right?"

"Yes, but Mary when we were talking, said that

Joseph, her husband, had been summoned to go to Bethlehem to register for the census when she was with child. While they were there, Jesus was born. She said they moved to Egypt for a while and then returned and settled in Nazareth."

"He grew up in Nazareth but was born in Bethlehem?"

Azan was shocked! "He *was* born in Bethlehem!"

"What difference does it make that he was born in Bethlehem?"

"The scripture says that the Messiah would be born in Bethlehem, but everyone thinks Jesus was born in Nazareth. I think he could be the Messiah."

"Be careful, Azan. You know how your father feels about false teachers."

"I will. I've been studying about the Messiah, so I don't make a wrong conclusion."

He was overjoyed and wanted to search out the truth about Jesus even more. He kept studying Scripture so much that Eliah started giving him a tough time about staying after school too long instead of going directly out to help with the sheep. But he was on a mission to find the truth.

One afternoon, he and Eliah were watching the sheep and Azan asked, "Do you think Jesus is the Messiah?"

"I don't know, but it wouldn't surprise me. He is becoming more well-known. I keep hearing stories about him healing and teaching. Why do you ask?"

"I have been studying the scriptures, and I'm beginning to believe that Jesus is the Messiah!"

"That's what you've been doing after school. You better watch out—your father will not be happy with you!"

"I know, but the more I find out, the more it looks true."

"Like what?"

"They call him a Nazarene, right?"

"Yes, he's from Nazareth."

"I found out he grew up in Nazareth but was born in Bethlehem. The scriptures say that the Messiah would come from Bethlehem."

"I thought he was born in Nazareth."

"Most people *think* he was born in Nazareth, but my mother was talking to the same woman that asked him to change the water into wine. She is Jesus' mother.

She said Jesus was born in Bethlehem."

"That doesn't prove anything."

"I know, but there are other things that point to him being the Messiah."

"I don't know about you, but if I were you, I would be careful talking about this in public. The Pharisees are looking for anyone talking about Jesus to silence them.

You may make it difficult for your father."

"I tried to discuss it with Father, but he gets sharp with me when I try to bring it up. My mother warned me also. She said, he is a leader and must abide by the rules of the Pharisees. This will not look good for him if my interest in Jesus is a topic of discussion in the Synagogue."

"She is right, you need to let this go."

"I can't. He *is* the Messiah."

From then on, he kept his thoughts to himself to avoid any conflict. But it didn't change how he felt about Jesus. He kept studying and trying to learn as much as he could to confirm for himself what he was beginning to believe. The more he read, the more he was convinced that Jesus was the Messiah.

CHAPTER 10

When Jesus went to Capernaum after his village rejected him, Azan heard many accounts concerning Jesus. He started writing down everything he heard. He kept it hidden so that his father would not see it. People in town were talkingr about him healing people, including casting out an unclean spirit from a man in the Synagogue.

In town, Azan came upon a group of people that were talking and heard them say Jesus' name. Azan drew close enough to hear what they were saying. One man said, "I witnessed the demon who cried out with a loud voice, saying, 'Let us alone! What have we to do with you, Jesus of Nazareth? Did you come to destroy us? I know you are the Holy One of God!'"

Another man said, "Even the demons think he is the Messiah!"

In town, some believed he was the Messiah, and others were adamant that he wasn't. The Pharisees where out more often walking in the town to see if they could catch people talking about Jesus. When the people saw them approaching, they dispersed. They wanted to catch people so they could reprimand them in public as an example.

On one occasion, there were two men who were arguing about Jesus in the center of town. One of the Pharisees went over to them, and in a very loud voice, said, "Do you see what is happening? This Jesus is causing an uprising. If you continue to talk about this Jesus, we will throw you out of the Synagogue. This Jesus is demon possessed; he has blasphemed against God. When are you going to listen to the authority of the Pharisees?"

Azan heard about men leaving their businesses and families to follow Jesus. His fame went throughout Galilee. People from all over were flocking to him to listen to him speak. The report was that the religious leaders were angry with Jesus and wanted to seize him to bring him to trial for blasphemy because he forgives sins and heals people. The leaders believed that God was the only one who could forgive and the only one who could heal.

∞

Azan continued to search scripture to see what they revealed about the coming Messiah. He wanted to find a connection between Jesus and the written word. He came to Deuteronomy 18:18. *'I will raise up a Prophet among their countrymen like you, and I will put my words in His mouth. And he shall speak to them all that I command him. It shall come about that whoever will not listen to my words which he shall speak in My name, I Myself will require it of him. But the prophet who speaks a word presumptuously My name which I have not commanded him to speak, or which he speaks in the name of other gods, that prophet shall die. You may say in your heart, "How will we know the word which the Lord has not spoken?'* He kept reading. *'When a prophet speaks in the*

name of the Lord, if the thing does not come about or come true, that is the thing the Lord has not spoken.'
I want to hear him speak for myself.

∾

Azan's mother put the evening meal on the table, and they all gathered to eat. They sat talking about their day when Yosef said, "I will be going to Capernaum tomorrow. Azan, I want you to come with me, we will be staying with my brother, Ephraim. We will leave early in the morning. I have some business there."

Heba asked, "How long will you be gone?"

"We will be gone several days. Medad will be managing the sheep while we're gone."

Azan was happy to go with him and looked forward to visiting his uncle Ephraim. *Uncle Ephraim doesn't look too much like father. He has dark eyes, but his hair and skin are lighter and he's a little shorter than father. He is two years younger, and he looks more like their father and my father looks more like their mother.*

I could talk to father about Jesus on our walk to

Capernaum. But I want this to be an enjoyable time with father while we are alone. I shouldn't mention Jesus.

Azan gathered up his belongings and made sure he had enough clothes for the trip before he went to bed.

∾

The sun was shining in the window, and Azan got up and dressed and went to the table to eat. Todros and Dobah were at the table.

He saw his parents talking outside the front door.

Mother looks concerned.

She looked at him and came into the house.

Meir came running in and got up on his bench. Azan wasn't sure what was going on and chose to be silent. He sat down to eat. Yosef came and joined them and prayed over the meal.

∞

They were securing their supplies on the donkey when Medad came to lead the sheep out to pasture. The men talked and then Medad headed over to the sheep pen.

∞

They said their goodbyes and left for Capernaum. The two of them walked along for a while.

I wonder what father was talking to mother about. They looked serious.

Azan decided to ask, "Do you mind me asking what the business is in Capernaum? Is that why mother looked concerned this morning?"

"I was telling your mother about Jesus, the man who is claiming to be the Son of God. The Pharisees are meeting with the leaders of Galilee to discuss it. I am standing for Cana. I want you to hear what they have to say. I know you are interested in this man. It would be best if you listened to the truth about him. I'm concerned that your interest in this Jesus will cause problems for us, and I was sharing my concern with your mother."

"How can we know the truth about him if we don't investigate it? I've been studying Scripture about the coming Messiah. I still have unanswered questions."

"I know you have. I talked to your Rabbi. He told me you have been spending a lot of time studying. You have been leaving the shepherding to Eliah a little too much. But I'm glad you are studying scripture. I want you to listen to what the

Pharisees have to say. They are the authority, and we are to take what they say seriously."

You know what will happen if your curiosity gets back to the Pharisees. It could put us all in jeopardy."

"Does this mean that you don't think it's possible for him to be the Messiah?"

"All I know is that we need the truth!"

"Did you know that Jesus was born in Bethlehem, not Nazareth?"

"Where did you hear that?"

"Mother was talking to Jesus' mother, Mary, at the wedding we went to. She said they went to Bethlehem for the census when she was with child, because that was her husband's town of origin. Mary had him while they were in Bethlehem. They went to Egypt for a while and then came back and settled in Nazareth."

"That doesn't prove that he is who he says he is. Let us see what the Pharisees have to say."

"Have you heard what Jesus has been doing all around Galilee?"

"Yes, I've heard he's been healing multitudes of people and casting out demons. The Pharisees are concerned that he will draw people away from our teachings and traditions. Our family has been following these traditions for generations, and I plan to continue in their footsteps."

"I wish I could listen to him teach so I can hear for myself."

"We must be careful, not to be deceived by a false prophet. You are still young and have more studying to do. How would you be able to discern his teachings? The Pharisees say he claims to be the Son of God. That is blasphemy!"

"Wouldn't it be worse for us if he is the Son of God, and we deny him?"

Yosef looked at him with contempt and said, "That is exactly what will get you in trouble. Enough for now, we need to listen to what the Pharisees have to say about all of this!"

For the rest of the trip, they walked in silence.

I wish father would be more open to discussing this in more depth with me. I have good reasons to believe that Jesus is the Messiah. I want so much to be able to listen to him teach and confirm what I believe.

Capernaum was sixteen miles, and it took them six and half hours to get there, including rest stops.

"It will be good to see Ephraim. I miss him. He is a good man."

Yosef said, "Yes, but I wish he would return to the Synagogue."

CHAPTER 11

T hey arrived in Capernaum and went to Ephraim's house that was situated in walking distance to the Sea of Galilee.

Ephraim was working in his shop next to his house and looked up.

"What are *you* two doing here? It's good to see you."

"I have business at the Synagogue tomorrow morning.
I hope we are not intruding."

"No, I'm glad to have you. How long will you be here?"

"Just a couple of days."

"Azan, you have grown since I saw you last. How is the family?"

"They're all doing good. How has business been for you?"

"To tell the truth, I can't keep up with all the orders that I have. But better that then not enough. Come inside and set your things down. I'm finished for the day."

"Heba sent some food so we wouldn't impose on you. Azan, will you take it out of the bag and set it out on the table?"

"Yes, Father."

Ephraim washed his hands and placed three plates on the table.

Azan arranged the food on separate plates in the middle of the table and they sat down.

"This looks good. I'm not much of a cook."

"Have as much as you want."

"So, what is this business all about at the Synagogue? I hear that the Pharisees from Jerusalem have arrived in town."

"It's about this new teacher named Jesus who has been creating concern in Jerusalem and in the region of Galilee. They are here to discuss it with the leaders from the area."

"I've heard about him; he has become the point of a lot of discussion among the people. He has been in Capernaum and people have been gathering to listen to him teach. Half of the people are convinced he is the Messiah, and the other half are saying he is a false teacher."

"The local leaders have warned the people about Jesus. They said that if anyone follows him, they will throw them out of the Synagogue."

They talked into the night, and Azan finally got tired and went to bed.

∾

Azan woke up, dressed, and rolled his bedding up and moved it to the side.

"Good morning, Ephraim."

"Good morning. There's some food on the table if you are hungry."

"Thank you, are you coming to the Synagogue with us?"

"No, I have work to do. You can tell me all about it later."

Yosef came in from outside and sat down next to Azan. "When you finish, please clear the table, and clean the dishes. Ephraim doesn't need to wait on us."

"Yes, Father, I will."

"Ephraim, I wish you would come with us to the Synagogue. You might want to hear what they say."

"I have an order that I need to complete today. You can tell me about it tonight."

Azan finished eating and started clearing the table.

Ephraim and Yosef went out to the shop. Azan finished his task and joined them.

"What are you working on, Ephraim?"

"I have an order of twenty-four hub rings for a man who makes and sells wagons. He needs all twenty-four by tomorrow morning so he can finish his carts. I have several more to make today to complete the order."

Yosef said, "We should leave now and go to the Synagogue."

"I'm ready."

The Synagogue was a ten-minute walk from Ephraim's house.

People were crowding into the room. They went inside and found a place to sit. The room was filled with chatter about what the Pharisees might say.

Then the High Priest stood up in front of everyone and hushed the room.

He said, "We have made the journey here to discuss the rumors of this man called Jesus. He has traveled around all of Galilee and Judea preaching false prophecy and claiming to be the Son of God. He and his followers do not observe the Sabbath. He has kept company with sinners and tax collectors. He does not follow our Jewish traditions and laws. He goes into our Synagogues and speaks blasphemies against God. We do not want our people to be deceived by his teachings. He heals people and casts out demons. But is he a demon himself?

"I am here to warn those who want to believe this man. If we find you discussing among yourselves what this man is doing and decide to follow him, we will throw you out of the Synagogue and ostracize you in the community. This is a serious matter, and we will not tolerate it."

The crowd listened intently; no one said anything against

what he said. After the meeting, the people filed out of the room and went their ways.

...

Yosef ushered Azan out of the room and to the town center. Yosef began talking with a group of men. Azan walked across to the marketplace and was looking at the different booths. He stopped in the shade and heard two men talking.

One man said, "I heard that this Jesus has been preparing for a sermon tomorrow on a nearby mount outside of town on the Korazim Plateau. People from all over are coming to listen to him speak. That is why so many people are here in Capernaum.

One of the other men said, "I heard him teach, and he spoke with authority and power. I do not know what to think about all of this. On the one hand, Jesus is believable, but the Pharisees make a good point. I don't want to go against the Jewish authority, but I want to hear what he has to say."

I would love to go listen to him tomorrow. I want to hear him speak and see if what he says is against Scripture or if he speaks the truth. But I know father would be furious with me.

Yosef came looking for Azan and said, "Let's get back to Ephraim's."

∞

That night as he lay down to sleep, he thought, *Should I risk fathers' anger and get up early and go to hear Jesus speak? I know Father will be terribly angry with me, but I want to go. I may not get another chance to hear him. I must know if what he says confirms scripture or goes against it.*

Azan could not sleep that night with the anxiety he felt. He was torn between wanting to hear Jesus and not wanting to anger his father. He made his decision. He got up before anyone else, grabbed some food off the table, and a water skin and set out. He saw groups of people walking out of town and followed them. He was worried about his father being angry with him, but he went anyway. *I know I will have to suffer the consequences.* After about an hour's journey, he saw multitudes of people gathered around a large mount sitting in the grass.

He made his way through the crowd and found a place to sit. He recognized the men that had been at the wedding standing next to Jesus. He moved closer to where Jesus was, so he could hear him speak.

Jesus turned and looked out at the multitude of people and smiled. Everyone became silent and watched in anticipation of what he would say. Azan remembered the feeling he had when Jesus smiled at him in Nazareth. He closed his eyes and prayed, "God, help me to understand who Jesus is. If he is your son, give me wisdom to know it in my heart."

They all sat down on the side of the mount, and he began to talk. "**Blessed are the poor in spirit, for theirs is the kingdom of heaven. Blessed are the gentle, for they shall inherit the earth. Blessed are those who hunger and thirst for righteousness, for they shall be satisfied. Blessed are the merciful, for they shall receive mercy. Blessed is those who hunger and thirst for righteousness, for they will be filled. Blessed is the merciful, for they will be shown mercy. Blessed are the pure in heart, for they shall see God. Blessed is the peacemaker, for they will be called children of God. Blessed are you when people insult you and persecute you, and falsely say all kinds of evil against you because of Me. Rejoice and be glad, for your reward in heaven is great; for in the same way, they persecuted the prophets who were before you.**"

He went on to say, "**But I say to you, love your enemies and pray for those who persecute you, so that you may be sons of your Father in heaven; He causes His sun to rise on**

the evil and the good and sends rain on the righteous and
the unrighteous."

He continued; *"You are the salt of the earth. But if the salt
has become tasteless, how can it be made salty again? It is no
longer good for anything, except to be thrown out and trampled
underfoot by men."*

"You are the light of the world. A city set on a hill
cannot be hidden. Nor does anyone light a lamp and put it
under a basket. But on a lampstand, and it gives light to
all who are in the house. Let your light shine before men
in such a way that they may see your good works and
glorify your

Father who is in heaven. Do not think that I came to
abolish the Law or the Prophets; I did not come to abolish
but to fulfill. For truly I say to you, until heaven and earth
pass away, not the smallest letter, or stroke shall pass from
the Law until all is accomplished. Whoever then annuls
one of the least of these commandments and teaches
others to do the same shall be called least in the kingdom
of heaven; but whoever keeps and teaches them, he shall
be called great in the kingdom of heaven. For I say to you
that unless your righteousness surpasses that of the
scribes and Pharisees you will not enter the kingdom of
heaven."

Azan was amazed at all that Jesus had said. He *did* teach
with authority like he had heard. He taught differently than the
teachers of the Law. Azan was so intrigued by everything he said
that he did not realize how late it had gotten. He knew he
needed to get back to his father even though he wanted to stay
and hear more. He knew he had to leave. But what
consequences was he about to face?

CHAPTER 12

He got up and started walking. He had been listening so intently that he had forgotten to eat. He reached into his bag and pulled out a piece of bread. He tried to remember what he had heard. *He came to fulfill the Law not to abolish it. He said that we should be humble, unlike the Pharisees who appear outwardly righteous. Does that mean their hearts may not be in the right place?*

Did he mean that righteousness was from God, not man? I found no fault in Jesus. He was humble, spoke with authority, and all the miracles he had performed showed his character. Jesus was amazing.

Jesus was teaching the word of God. The words he had learned in studying the scrolls in school. This changes everything. This doesn't go against the scripture. This is confirming it, Jesus is the Messiah. I know it in my heart.

∾

It was after dark when he reached his uncle's house. Ephraim was outside and saw Azan approaching. He took him aside and told him that his father was terribly angry with him. He looked up and saw his father in the doorway.

Ephraim went inside and his father walked toward him. Before Azan could apologize, his father said, "You went to listen to this Jesus, didn't you? You know how I feel about this. We will talk later. We leave in the morning."

Azan rolled out his bed and laid down. He had a knot in his stomach from the anxiety he felt. Tears welled up in his eyes. I know I disappointed father. How can I make things right with him? I wish he could understand why I had to go listen to Jesus. I will try to talk to him on the way home."

∾

"Thank you for your hospitality, Ephraim."

"You're welcome, have a safe walk home."

"Goodbye, Ephraim."

Ephraim placed is hand on Azan's shoulder and looked at him with sorrow. "Goodbye, Azan."

The walk started quietly, and Azan was feeling horrible.

Yosef walked ahead of Azan and would not look at him. Azan was trying to think of what to say to him. He wanted to share his joy in knowing that Jesus was the Messiah, but he knew now was not the time.

After miles of silence, they sat down in the shade. Azan got the courage to speak.

"I know you're disappointed in me. Please try to listen to me."

Yosef finally looked at Azan.

"You know that I have been studying Scripture all this time. I have been searching through the word of God to see what it says about the Messiah. I needed to hear what Jesus had to say so I could check it against what I've learned. How can we know if he is or is not the Messiah unless we understand what he is saying and compare it with Scripture? That is what I was doing."

Yosef looked down and then up at Azan. "Don't you realize that you are jeopardizing my position as a leader in our community? They will kick us out of the Synagogue. We will not be welcome in our own community. This Jesus is a mere man who claims to be the Son of God. If you continue this path, you will not be welcome in my house."

Azan gasped.

"I cannot allow you to put not only me, but all of us in jeopardy. Do you understand?"

"I understand!"

Azan was angry and hurt that his father would say such a thing. *Would he really cast me out?*

How would he keep quiet when he wanted to shout from the rooftops that Jesus was the Messiah?

We've been waiting for the Messiah to come and rescue us from the Roman occupation. Repeatedly, I have heard that he would come in power and might and defeat the Romans and set the Jews free from their rule. Never in my studies have I seen anything about him coming with vengeance. I'll continue to study to learn more. The Messiah is here. Father and the Pharisees can't see that it's him, the Messiah.

He prayed as he trailed behind his father. *Dear God, thank you for showing me that Jesus is your Son. I want my father to know that for himself. Please open his eyes so he can see who Jesus is. Amen.*

The journey seemed long after their discussion. They didn't speak all the way home. Azan felt crushed.

CHAPTER 13

At dusk, they arrived home. Azan's mother was happy to see them until she saw Yosef's face. She could tell that something had happened on the trip. Her instinct was to let it go.

So, she said, "You two must be hungry. Let me fix you something."

She broke off a piece of bread and placed it on a plate with fruit and handed it to Azan. He didn't feel comfortable in the house with his father, so he took the food and went outside to eat but he wasn't hungry.

Dobah was happy that he was home and came and sat next to him and asked, "Why is Father upset?"

"It's a long story for another time."

She began telling him everything that had happened while they were gone. She babbled on about Meir not letting Todros have the toy that mother made him. She said, "He took it away from Todros and would not give it back. Meir had both toys she made for them." She continued but his mind wandered, *What is going to happen? What will father do, will he eventually forgive me? I hope so.*

Azan looked up and he could see his father in the house at

the table with Meir, who was trying to get his attention, but Father didn't respond to his tapping on his leg. Todros came out and sat against the house with the toy he was able to get back from Meir. He played with the toy until Meir couldn't engage father and came outside. He saw Todros with the toy and went over to take it from him.

"Meir, let Todros have his toy. Come over here for a minute."

He came over, and Azan picked him up and set him on his lap and tickled him. Meir wiggled and laughed.

"Let me see the toy mother made for *you*."

Meir jumped down to search for it. Azan could see him looking around the house until he lost interest and found his way to Mother's lap. Todros looked up and smiled at Azan.

He sat outside till it was dark, and he finally went inside.

His father looked at him and said, "You will go and tend the sheep tomorrow."

"What about school?"

In a stern voice, "I said, you will go and tend the sheep!" Azan went and laid down on his bed, tears flowed down his face, and he turned toward the wall so no one would see. He did not know how else to react to this. *Is Father going to keep me out of school for good? I wanted to study so I can learn more.*

∼

Azan woke up and quietly, dressed and went directly out to get the sheep. He opened the sheep pen and started herding them out one by one. Once he had them all out of the pen, he got behind them and started encouraging them down the road. When he got them to pasture, he sat down on a log. He spent the morning thinking about Jesus and his father.

He prayed. *God, please help me do what is right in your eyes. I don't know what to do. I want to honor Jesus and my father. How can I do both?* He kept going over the things Jesus had said.

'Blessed are you when people insult you, persecute you and falsely say all kinds of evil against you because of me. Rejoice and be glad, for your reward in heaven is great, for in the same way they persecuted the prophets who were before you.'

It's hard to be joyful when father is so angry with me.

He saw someone coming in the distance and it was his mother.

She approached him and sat down next to him. "I brought you some food. I know you didn't have anything before you left this morning. What happened between you and your father?"

"He is angry with me because I snuck away to listen to Jesus."

"Didn't you know that he would get angry? Why didn't you ask him if you could go?"

"I knew he would be angry with me, but I also knew he would not allow me to go if I asked him. The Pharisees made it powerfully clear that if anyone follows Jesus they would be cast out.

"All I wanted to do was to hear him teach so I could know if he is who he says he is. I wanted to compare what I have learned in Scripture to see if he could be the Messiah. I understand that this would put us in a threatening situation with the Pharisees, but I had to know if he is the Messiah or not. I didn't think I would get another chance to hear him. I asked father, wouldn't it be worse for us to deny him if he is from God?"

He looked at her with tears flowing down his face, "Mother, after listening to him, Jesus *is* the Messiah. There is something extraordinary about him. I have a deep sense that it is true. What do I do?"

His mother looked at him with sorrow and said, "I wish I could make things right between you and your father. I don't know if this man is who he claims to be or not. How can we know for sure? Like your father has said, he could be a false teacher. Your father has been studying scripture his whole life. I would hope he would know if this man were true or not."

"I know what you are saying, but I truly believe he is the Messiah, I just know it."

"But you know that your father will not allow anything to interfere with his position. It has been handed down through the generations to be leaders of the Jewish Law. He will not allow his status to be compromised. He is required to follow what the Pharisees think about Jesus. I suggest you not talk to anyone about this and let him calm down. I don't know if he will but, just do what he says."

"I'm sorry about all of this. Please forgive me. I will try my best to obey him, but I can't put Jesus out of my mind. I just cannot!"

Heba put her arms around him and just held him for a while. He felt comfort in her arms, but it was only temporary.

CHAPTER 14

Azan went out each day that week to tend the sheep.
Upon their return from Capernaum, his father
told him not to talk to anyone. He told him that
Eliah would not be tending the sheep with him. He didn't want
him talking to Eliah. He felt isolated and depressed. He would
sit outside the house after bringing the sheep home and go into
the house only to go to bed. His mother tried to get him to
come in to eat, but he couldn't sit at the table with his father.
He couldn't look him in the eye.

After a week of being isolated, Azan was feeling lost and
alone.

One evening, Dobah came outside to him and said, "Father
and Mother were talking, and I overheard them saying that they
are sending you to stay with Uncle Ephraim in Capernaum.
Why are they sending you away?"

Azan's heart sank. He could not believe that they were
sending him away.

"I don't know, Dobah. I suppose I deserve it."

"What did you do?"

His father stepped out the door and said, "Azan, I need you
to come into the house."

Yosef said, "I have been giving this problem we have concerning Jesus a lot of thought. We cannot go on like this. I can't keep you isolated for long. I want you to denounce this Jesus at once and not talk about him or seek to follow him, or I will have no choice but to send you to stay with Ephraim. If people find out what you have done, it will not go well for any of us. Will you denounce this Jesus right now?"

Azan was shocked. "I know you are worried about the Pharisees, and I don't want to cause you any trouble."

"You won't if you do as I say."

"Father, please try to understand!"

"No, *you* need to understand. I will not tolerate this in my house!"

"Father, I love you and I want to respect your wishes, but I cannot forget what I have heard and seen. I cannot denounce Jesus."

They stared at each other, neither wanting to surrender.

"Then you are to leave this house at once! Pack what you need and leave. You are not to return until I say so. I talked to Ephraim when we were there and told that I might be sending you to him. Do not go through town, take the road outside of town. Do not talk to anyone." He turned and went outside.

Azan hung his head and went to gather the things he thought he might need. He gathered some clothes and put them into his bag. Then he saw his writings about Jesus in the shelf next to his bed hidden under some clothes and put it in the bag and closed it. He looked at his sling shot but decided he didn't want it. He looked over at Todros' bed and walked over and laid it on his bed. He rolled up his bed and looked around the room and his heart sunk. *I won't be seeing Dobah, Todros, and Meir for a while. And Mother! But, how long?*

Then he saw the book that his father gave him at his Bar Mizpah, sitting on the table next to his bed. *I don't deserve this —I'll give it back to father.* He took it into his parent's room and laid it on his father's side of the bed.

Heba had ushered the other children outside to give him some space. She was waiting in the living area for him when he came out of the room. He went to his mother and hugged her. He looked into her eyes and saw that she had been crying.

"I'll be okay. God is with me! Remember that!"

They went outside and he hugged Dobah, Todros, and Meir and told them to behave. He saw his father out by the sheep pen staring out toward the hills.

His mother said, "Oh wait I have something for you." She went into the house and came running out, handed him a bag of food, and hugged him once more with tears running down her face.

Hold it together Azan, don't make the children cry. I can't look at Dobah or I will lose it. He hugged his mother one last time and left.

He walked the outskirts of town like his father asked and didn't encounter anyone. He had walked for two hours until the sun had set, and it was getting dark. He stopped by a wooded area and rolled his pad out under a tree. He opened the bag his mother had given him and looked inside. He took a piece of her bread out to eat but he just looked at it, smelled it and returned it to the bag. He laid down and sobbed as he thought about his fathers' words. All he could do is pray.

Father God, please help me in my time of need. I know why I had to choose between your son and my father. I know in my heart who Jesus is. Please, help my father know who he is. Will I be staying with Ephraim for long? I will miss my family. How can my father cast me out like this? He just doesn't understand.

∞

Birds chirping woke him up as the sun was coming up and he felt the sun's warmth on his back. He walked a couple of hours and sat down in the grass to rest and prayed. *God, I remember what Jesus said, "**Love your enemies and pray for***

those who persecute you, so that you may prove yourselves
to be sons of your Father who is in heaven."

Father God, help me to love those that do not understand the
truth. Help me to follow you. Help them to know the truth.

He suddenly felt a sense of peace that he had never felt
before. He started to gather his things when he saw a young
man walking by. The man got a pebble in his sandal, so he
stopped and reached down to remove it. Azan caught up with
him. He looked to be in his mid-twenties, messy long brown
shoulder length hair with brown eyes.

"Mind if I walk with you?"

"I would like your company, where are you headed?"

"To my uncle's house in Capernaum. Where are *you* going?"

"I'm going to Capernaum also. Do you live in
Capernaum?"

"No, my family lives in Cana. I'm going to stay with my
uncle for a while."

"Problems at home?"

"You could say that!"

"That's too bad. I hope you can resolve it."

"So do I!"

"Mind if I ask what the problem is?"

"My father and I have differing opinions on our beliefs. He
is a Jewish leader, and I am trying to seek the truth about the
Messiah, and he will have no part of it. He is worried what the
Pharisees will do if they find out that I am seeking him."

"Oh, you mean Jesus?"

Azan looked at him and said, "Yes, my father stands with the
Pharisees, and I am threatening his position by looking into
Jesus."

"What do you know about Jesus?"

"I have encountered him on several occasions, the most
recent was just outside of Capernaum about a week ago. We
were visiting my uncle.

He was speaking and I left my uncle's house and went to

hear him without my father's permission. My father was furious, but I needed to hear him. I wanted to know the truth."

"I have been with Jesus. You are right to seek him. Are you going to be in Capernaum long?"

"I don't think I will be going home anytime soon."

"I would like to spend some time with you in Capernaum. I'm a fisher, maybe you could join me for a day of fishing."

"I would like that; my uncle lives close to the water. I could meet you there."

"Let's meet tomorrow, at the light of dawn, at Kfar Nahum beach."

"I'll be there."

CHAPTER 15

Azan arrived at Ephraim's house and went to the door.

Ephraim looked up. "Azan, what are you doing here. Are you alone?"

"Yes, it's just me."

"Something happened! Your father is still angry with you, right? He said he might be sending you here."

"Yes, more than angry. I hope you don't mind."

"I'm sorry to hear that. You're welcome here. You can stay however long you need to. Come in."

"I can help around here for my keep."

"I'll find things for you to do."

"You can stay in the house or there is a loft over the shop if you would like some privacy."

"I think I would like the loft. I don't want to interrupt *your* privacy."

"I've been alone so long—it will be nice to have someone around for a change."

"I have an invitation to go fishing tomorrow at Kfar Nahum beach if you don't mind. I will be gone all morning."

"No, I don't mind. Bring home a fish or two from your catch!"

"I will if we catch any."

"Who are you going with?"

"Andrew, I met him on my way here. He lives here in Capernaum. I'll be meeting him early at Kfar Nahum beach in the morning. His father owns a boat, and his two sons help him with the fishing."

∾

Azan shared the food that his mother had sent with Ephraim.

They sat at the table and Ephraim asked, "So what happened after you left here?"

"Father didn't talk to me most of the way home. We stopped to rest, and I tried to explain why I went to hear Jesus speak. I told him that I wanted to compare what Jesus said with the scriptures. I asked him, 'How can we know whether Jesus is who he says he is, if we don't listen to him?' He said to me, 'You are putting the family in jeopardy and said he wouldn't tolerate it.'

"After we got home, he wouldn't allow me to talk to anyone, and had me spend my days with the sheep. I couldn't go to school or even be around my friend. Then, he asked me to denounce Jesus."

He looked at Ephraim, "I couldn't. I know that Jesus is telling the truth, he *is* from God. He's the Messiah."

"Yes, you have angered him. But what makes you think he is the Messiah?"

"He speaks with authority, yet he is humble. He quotes scripture like he wrote it. It was amazing listening to him. Then you have John the Baptist who when seeing Jesus said, 'Behold the lamb of God, who takes away the sin of the world.' I've been trying to understand what he meant by the Lamb of God, and it somehow relates to the lambs we use in the sacrifices to cover our sins. We were in Nazareth and went to the Synagogue and he stood and read from Isaiah 61:1 and then proclaimed, 'Today this scripture is fulfilled in your hearing.'

"I know he is the Messiah; I couldn't denounce him. That would be like denouncing God."

"Your father takes his responsibilities seriously. He means well, and I'm sure this is hard on him also. Let's pray that he finds a way to get over his anger and reconcile with you."

"I hope so. I didn't want to disappoint him, but I just had to know if Jesus is who he says he is."

Later, Azan went out to the shop and climbed up the ladder to the loft. "Oh, I need a broom, it's dusty up here."

He found the broom and started sweeping. He arranged his bed and found a wooden box that served as a table. He turned it on its side and placed a smaller box in it for a shelf.

This is a good place to keep my writings. This is going to be my home for a while, I just don't know how long.

∾

Azan was excited to go fishing and went to the beach at first light. He found Andrew by the shore next to a boat.

Andrew saw him and said, "Oh, Azan, you made it!"

"Yes, I'm looking forward to this."

"Great. Help me grab this net and put it in the boat."

Azan walked over, grabbed a corner, and tried to lift it. "Wow, this is heavy."

He struggled, but he finally got his end of the net into the boat.

"It's just you and me today. Simon Peter, my brother, is spending time with his wife. Get in, and I will push off!"

Azan got into the boat.

"Take the oar and help me move this beast!"

Azan grabbed the oar, put the tip into the water and pulled the oar back a little hard and splashed Andrew in the back of the boat.

"Whoa, now that's one way to wake up!"

"Oh, sorry!"

"Try putting it in the water and push the top of the handle forward while the tip pushes back. Try it a couple of times. You'll get it."

"I haven't been in a boat before."

"That's okay—you have to start somewhere."

It was a little awkward at first, but he got the hang of it. They were a reasonable distance from the shore and Andrew dropped the anchor.

He said, "Take hold of the end of the net like this"—he gathered the net about a foot from his end— "and when I tell you, throw your end of the net into the water as far as you can throw it."

Azan watched how Andrew gathered his end and tried to copy him.

He said, "On the count of three, pull it back and then throw it with all your strength."

Azan pulled it back and then threw it forward and let go but almost went in with it.

Andrew just laughed and said, "I had the shower, but you almost had the bath."

They sat down to wait, and Andrew spoke up. "So, you want
to seek Jesus?"

Azan got tears in his eyes and said, "Yes, even at the risk of my father disowning me. You said that you have been with Jesus?"

"I will tell you a story. I heard about a man named
John the Baptist and went to see what he was all about.
I started following him and listened to him preach."

"You knew John the Baptist?"

"Yes. I followed him for a while. Then this man came to the river and asked John to baptize him. John told him, '**I need to be baptized by you, and yet you have come to me?**'

The man replied, '**Let it be so now; it is proper for us to do this to fulfill all righteousness.**' Then John baptized him.

When he came up out of the water, a voice from heaven said, 'This is my Son, whom I love; with him, I am well pleased.'

"I heard it very clearly, but others thought it was thunder. The strange thing was, that there were no clouds in the sky.

"Time had passed, and I was with John by the water, and he saw Jesus approaching and said, 'Behold! The lamb of God who takes away the sin of the world!'

"My friend and I followed Jesus. He turned to us and asked us what we were seeking. We asked him where he was staying. He said, '**Come and see.**'

"We stayed with him the entire day. Later, I went to find my brother, Peter. I told him we have found the Messiah!"

"You believe he is the Messiah?"

He chuckled and continued. "I brought Simon to Jesus. Jesus changed his name to Peter. He said it meant 'stone.'

Since then, others began to follow him. There are twelve of us now."

"Where is Jesus right now?"

"After speaking to multitudes of people, performing miracles, and walking all over Galilee, he went into the wilderness to be alone for a while. We never know when he will return when he goes off by himself."

"I thought you looked familiar; I saw you with him at the wedding in Cana."

"You were at that wedding?"

"Yes, I saw him turn the water into wine. I couldn't believe what I saw. My friend and I saw the servants fill the waterpots with water. We saw the headwaiter taste it and he complimented the groom for saving the best wine for last. That was the first time I saw him. You have spent time with him, please tell me more about him."

"Have you got all day?"

"I think you have a captive audience."

Andrew continued, "Jesus is here to fulfill the law, not to abolish it."

"I heard him teach that, at the Sermon on the Mount."

"He teaches that the scriptures point to him. He has come to set people free from sin. If we believe in him, he says we will be set free from sin and have eternal life. He has the power to heal people. The blind, the lame, people that are demon possessed, and those that are deaf. When people hear he is around, they bring their sick to him to heal them."

"I saw him healing people in the Temple during the Passover. The Pharisees didn't like that happening in front of the people. I saw them talking and pointing to him. They confronted him and he responded and then left. They don't like that people are believing in him."

"The Pharisees want him to go away. He is threatening their authority over the people. They want to keep control over the masses. They have not been able to touch him so far. He has power over them and has walked right through them and nothing happens."

"He did that in Nazareth. They led him out of town to push him off a cliff after he spoke in the Synagogue. He walked right through them; they didn't even try to touch him."

"We are worried that they may try to arrest him. We want to protect him, but he tells us not to worry. He says he does what his father wills."

Andrew's attention was brought back to fishing. "Let's pull the net in and see what we have. Grab the net like this and pull it into the boat."

Azan grabbed it and tried to pull it in, but it was even heavier than before because it was now soaking wet.

"Come on, pull harder, you can do it."

They got the net into the boat and Azan said, "Look we *did* catch fish. Is this a good catch?"

"It's not bad, I've seen a lot better, but I've also seen a lot worse. Let's head back to shore."

Azan was distracted by the fish jumping around at his feet.

"Come on, keep rowing."

CHAPTER 16

Waiting for them on the shore was an older man with white hair and beard who was a little stooped over and looked a little weathered.

"Hello there. What kind of day did you have?"

"We've had worse days. About thirty-five or so."

"This is Azan—the boy I told you about."

"Hello, Azan."

"Azan, this is my father, Jonah."

"Hello, glad to meet you."

"Father, Peter and I are traveling so much. I thought maybe Azan could help you with the fishing."

"I don't know much, but I could learn."

"I could use some help. Can you be here tomorrow? I will pay for your time."

"I'll be here. Thank you for the opportunity!"

He jumped at the chance to earn a little extra money.

"We won't be around for a while. When Jesus gets back, we are touring Galilee. I will check in on you when we come back through Capernaum."

"Thank you for your kindness and for inviting me to fish with you."

They gathered the fish and took them to the market. Azan asked, "Would you mind if I took a couple of fish home to my uncle?"

"Not at all. Help yourself."

∞

Azan settled into a routine of fishing and helping Ephraim in his blacksmith shop, sweeping, and keeping things organized.

He was comfortable with Ephraim and enjoyed his company. In the evenings, they would sit and talk about things.

"I'm sorry you lost your wife and baby. That must have been extremely hard for you."

"It was the hardest thing in my life, losing her and the infant. It has been three years now. I still miss her."

"I'm so sorry that happened."

"One day at a time, right?"

"I would like to learn your trade. Can you teach me?"

"You'll have a lot to learn."

"I am willing."

Ephraim was a humble man and did not follow all the traditions as strictly as Azan's father. He was able to talk to him about anything and even discuss Jesus with him.

Azan didn't try to go to the Synagogue but missed being able to hear and study the Scriptures. He still had unanswered questions.

In the quiet of the night up in the loft, he thought about his family. *God, I pray that you would open my father's eyes to see the truth about Jesus. I want a good relationship with him, please make it possible. Please open father's heart so he can see who Jesus really is. I miss my Mother, Dobah, Todros, and Meir. I miss Father also. He buried his face in his bed and sobbed.*

After early morning fishing trips with Jonah, he worked in the shop, learning what he could. Ephraim was a good teacher.

∾

It was the weekend, and he went to the marketplace to buy some food for the house. He watched an older lady who was buying rice. She took out a small bag and emptied the coins into her hand and said, "I'm sorry. I don't have enough."

Azan heard her and walked over to her and asked the merchant, "How much more are you asking?"

He looked annoyed and said, "She is short two coins."

Azan took out what he had with him and gave the man two coins.

"Here, I will make up the difference."

She started to protest, but Azan said, "No, please let me do this for you."

She was surprised, looked him over and said, "Thank you, but you don't have to do that."

"It's my pleasure. Please accept my gift."

"Thank you. You are kind."

The merchant handed her the bag of rice, and with the weight of it she almost dropped it and tried to hoist it back up to her waist.

"That looks heavy. Can I carry it for you? Where are you going?"

"My home is just around the corner."

"Let me carry it to your home for you."

"You're a nice young man. I appreciate your help. You're not from around here, are you?"

"No, but I'm staying with my uncle for a while."

"Well, it's nice to meet you. I'm Ana."

"I'm Azan. Nice to meet you too."

They arrived at her home, and an old man met her at the door.

He looked Azan over and said, "Who is this?"

"Hello, my name is Azan. Is this your wife?"

"Yes. Who are you?"

"I noticed her in the market, and she was struggling with the weight of this bag, and I offered to carry it for her."

The man looked at him and said, "Well, thank you," and took the bag.

The woman said, "Thank you again, Azan."

The man motioned for her to come in and she went in.

From then on, Azan had a soft heart for those in need and would look for opportunities to help.

Encountering Jesus had changed him. He remembered what Jesus said at the Sermon on the Mount. *'Let your light shine before others, that they may see your good deeds and glorify your Father in Heaven.'*

Over the course of time in Capernaum, Azan gained skill in his fishing and in the shop under Ephraim's guidance.

One day, he was helping in the workshop thinking, *I've been in Capernaum for a year and a half, and I haven't heard anything from Mother or Father. Are they just going to leave me here indefinitely? My fourteenth birthday is next month. I don't care about my birthday, but I would like to go to the Passover this year. I wonder if Ephraim will go with me. It might be possible for me to at least see Mother in Jerusalem.*

"Ephraim, are you going to the Passover? If you are, can I come with you?"

"I don't think I will be able to go this year. I have more than a month's worth of work scheduled, and I won't get it all done by then."

"I understand. I was hoping to see Mother. I miss her and my siblings and my father."

"You need to be cautious around your father."

"Yes, I know. It has been almost two years since I've seen them."

"I know you miss them. I'm sure they miss you too."

Azan continued with his routine. Fishing with Jonah in the mornings and working in the shop in the afternoons.

One morning, out on the lake, he said, "Jonah, I heard that Jesus and the others are in town. Have you seen them?"

"Yes, I visited with them yesterday. Peter told of a centurion from Capernaum who sent some Jewish elders to Him when he was just leaving Cana, requesting Him to come to Capernaum and save the life of his highly favored slave who was sick and about to die. Peter said that men pleaded with him saying, he is worthy for you to grant him this, because he loves our nation and has built us a synagogue here in Capernaum. Jesus went with them, but before he could get to the centurion's house, the centurion sent word to tell Jesus, 'Don't trouble yourself, since I am not worthy to have you come under my roof.'

"Peter said that the centurion didn't consider himself worthy to come to Jesus himself. But asked that Jesus say the word, and his servant would live.

"When Jesus heard this, he turned to the crowd following him and said, '*I say to you, not even in Israel have I found such great faith.*'

"They said that they returned to the house and found the slave in good health. He didn't even have to be there to heal the man. The news of this is spreading all over Judea."

"Are they going to be here long?"

"No, they leave tomorrow for a town called Nain, south of here."

"Do you think I can see them before they leave?"

"They are staying in the olive grove at the southeast end of town if you want to see them."

After hauling in their catch, they sold them at the market, and Azan ran home. He found Ephraim in the house.

"Ephraim, there you are. Taking a break?"

"Yes, I needed to eat something. Done fishing for today?"

"Yes, I heard that Jesus is in town. Would you mind if I went to see him and the disciples before they leave town tomorrow? I can make up my time in the shop on the weekend if that would help. Do you want to come with me?"

"Hmm, you know, I think I would like to come. I'd like to see Jesus for myself. We can both work on the weekend."

Azan grabbed a piece of bread off the table and handed a piece to Ephraim, and the two of them set off on foot.

"Can we stop at the market so I can get a few things to take to them?"

"Okay, what are you going to get?"

"A couple of loaves of bread and fruit. They sometimes don't have the means to buy food."

They stopped at the market and then found them at the end of town, off the road in the shade of the olive trees.

Andrew got up when he saw them approaching.

"Azan, nice to see you. Who is this with you?"

"This is Ephraim, my uncle. We brought you something for your journey. Jonah said you are leaving tomorrow."

Jesus stood up and walked over. "Andrew, please introduce me to your friends."

"This is Azan, the boy I told you about. The one who is fishing with our father."

"Azan, it's nice to meet you. Thank you for helping Jonah. I'm sure he appreciates your help. Ephraim, nice to meet you also."

"Jonah is a nice man, I enjoy him. I brought you some food for your trip." Azan was trembling with excitement.

"You can hand it to Mary over there. Thank you for your generosity."

Mary got up and took the food, bowed her head, and said, "Thank you."

"Come and sit for a while."

"We were just talking about John the Baptist. As I was saying, you know he sent men to come and ask me if I am the one who is to come, or should we look for someone else? I said to them, 'Go and report to John the things you have seen and heard: The blind receives their sight, the lame walk, those with skin disease are healed, the deaf hear, the dead are raised, and the poor are told the good news.' I told them to tell him that anyone who is not offended because of me is blessed. I was explaining to my disciples that John is more than a prophet. I will repeat what I said to them, This is the one that it is written about: '**Look, I am sending My messenger ahead of you, Who will prepare Your way before You.**' This was speaking of John.

"Among those born of women, no one is greater than John, but the least in the kingdom of God is greater than he.

The Pharisees and experts in the law have rejected the plan of God for themselves. They think they are righteous, but those baptized with the Spirit are righteous. John said, 'I baptize with water for repentance. But after me comes one who is more powerful than I, whose sandals I am not worthy to carry. He will baptize you with the Holy Spirit.'"

When Jesus was done talking, they left to return home.

∞

Walking back home that night, Ephraim said, "I can now see why you believe this Jesus is the Messiah. I have never heard anyone speak like him. He *is* amazing. Thank you for inviting me along."

"Does that mean that you believe in Him—that He is the Messiah?"

Looking at Azan, he said, "I have no reason to think otherwise. Everything you have told me, and the things you have read from your writings, all make sense now after hearing Him."

Azan looked at him and smiled and hugged him. His heart was leaping inside his chest.

CHAPTER 17

It was a week before Passover. Azan was getting anxious about wanting to make the trip to Jerusalem.

"Ephraim, are you sure you can't go to the Passover?"

"I can't make it this year, I'm sorry."

"Is Jonah going? Ask if you can make the trip with him."

"He has already said he isn't going this year."

"Do you know of anyone else that might be going? I would feel more comfortable if you had someone to go with."

"I might, I'll ask around."

After Azan and Jonah brought the fish to the market the next day, he lingered in town to see if anyone he knew was going to the Passover.

Who do I know that might be going? I know a few people, but most of them are older and not able to make the trip. I wonder if Amos is going. He has his booth, but he may be planning to go.

Amos was a merchant he had befriended through Jonah. He was kind to Azan, and they had spent time talking and getting to know each other. He was a short, stocky man. He had kind eyes and was soft-spoken.

"Good morning, Amos!"

"Good morning, Azan. What can I help you with today?"

"Ephraim asked if I would buy a couple of loafs of bread. We are completely out."

"What would you like?

"The flat bread for sure, and a loaf of the seasoned bread. The sweet galette bread is one of my favorites. Do you have the kind with honey and dates?"

"Yes. You are lucky—it's my last two. Let me wrap them up for you. What are you going to do with yourself the rest of the day?"

Azan paid him and said, "I need to find someone who is going to the Passover. Ephraim has too much work and will not be able to go this year. He said he would be more comfortable if I went with someone."

"I know you fish with Jonah. What about him?"

"He has decided not to go."

"I didn't think I was going to be able to leave my booth for that long, but my wife, Maya, our son Luke, and I decided to go after all. It will be a short trip. I cannot leave my business for long. I have a family friend to fill in for me, but he can only manage the booth for a short while. We can't be gone more than ten days. We will have only two days in Jerusalem to celebrate the Passover. But you are welcome to come with us."

"You wouldn't mind? I'm hoping to see my mother in Jerusalem."

"No, not at all."

"Thank you. I appreciate it very much. I won't be any trouble," he said excitedly.

"We will leave from here on Monday before Passover. We'll be staying with my brother and his wife in the upper city. Are you comfortable going through Samaria? It's the shorter of the two routes."

"Yes, my family and I went the Samarian route two years ago. We stayed overnight, close to the stone outposts, with a large group of other pilgrims for safety."

"Yes, that is the safest thing to do. The Samaritans can be

unwelcoming, to say the least. We'll meet here at the booth at sunup, and we'll start off. My son Luke will enjoy having your company."

Azan saw Ana and her husband walking up. "Good morning, Azan. Nice to see you today." She had become good friends with Azan after his kindness to her. Her husband, John, was a serious man and didn't talk much.

"Good morning, Ana. Are you two out shopping today?"

"No, we are going to visit a friend, and John has business to tend to. What brings you to town?"

"I came to get bread for my uncle and me. I'm just heading back there now."

"Well, it was nice to see you. I hope to see you again soon."

∾

Walking back to Ephraim's, he thought, *I will have to be careful not to cause any trouble for Mother. If I could find where they are staying, I could set up a time and place to meet with her away from Father. I wish I could meet with him, but I don't know if it is possible. Jerusalem is a large city, and I won't have much time. I know there are no guarantees. God, thank you for making a way for me to see Mother.*

Azan was anxious, waiting for the week to end so they could start the journey to Jerusalem.

∾

We leave for Jerusalem tomorrow. Let's see what I should take. Looking through his clothes, he thought, *I think I'll take two tunics and an extra cloak. There won't be much shade, so I'll take an extra head covering. That should be enough.*

The morning came, and he packed up his bag with his clothes and some food. He rolled up his bed roll put a tie around it, leaving a loop so he could carry it over his shoulder.

"Ephraim, I'm leaving. I'll be back in ten days."

"Okay, make sure you let Amos know where you are at all times, and I'll see you when you return. I hope you get to visit with your mother."

"Thank you, God willing."

∾

He walked as fast as he could to Amos' booth. They were there waiting for him. Amos was giving last minute instructions to his friend.

"Good morning, Azan! We're glad you are joining us. Are you ready for a long walk?"

"Good morning! Yes, I'm ready."

Luke came up to him and started talking and did not stop. He was eleven and stood up to Azan's shoulders. He reminded Azan of Meir, just older. Same exuberant personality.

He asked every question he could think of about Azan's family, where they lived, why he was in Capernaum, why wasn't he going to school? And the list went on and on.

Azan tried to be patient with him, and he was ready for quiet when they sat down to rest and eat. Azan ate a bit of food he brought and went to the shade on the other side of the tree, laid down, and closed his eyes. He sensed Luke walking up to him—but he kept his eyes closed—then he heard him walk away.

God, he prayed, *please allow me to see my mother. I know you can do anything. If it is your will, make it so.*

Amos put Luke in charge of the donkey, which kept him busy.

"How is Ephraim doing?" Amos asked. "He has kept to himself since he lost his wife and infant. I know it has been hard on him."

"He keeps himself busy in the shop. We talk about everything, and he seems okay. I enjoy being with him. He's a good man. He has been teaching me his trade in blacksmithing. I do that in the afternoons when I'm done fishing with Jonah."

"I'm glad you have him. What about your family?"

"My father and I don't agree completely on our beliefs, and it's good to be apart for a while. I've been praying about it. I'm trusting God to make a way for us to come back together."

"Azan, you are a good boy. I see how generous you are with the older people in town and how you occupy the children while their mother's shop. You are humble and kind. Your father will come around, I'm sure of it."

"Thank you! I sure hope so."

"Do you have a plan on how to find your mother?" "Jerusalem is a large city. It will be challenging to find her in the short amount of time we have. But I am hopeful. I will look for her at the place we stayed before. If she's not there, I will have to walk around and hope I find her or someone who knows her."

"I hope you get a chance to see her while we're there. I'm sure she misses you too."

Luke started complaining. "How long do I have to hold on to this donkey?"

"I'll take him for a while."

"Thanks. Here, take him. Father said that you fish. I always wanted to fish. Can I come with you sometime?"

"I'll see what I can do. It's not my boat, so I will have to ask the owner."

Luke got quiet as his energy waned in the heat of the day. He caught up with his mother and walked with her.

Azan spent the time praying and singing to himself. He smiled as he thought about Ephraim becoming a believer in Jesus. His demeaner changed when he thought about his father. If only *he* would believe.

They reached Beth Shan, paid for a place for the night, and rested. Azan volunteered to water the donkey, then they sat around, eating and talking.

Luke came over to Azan and said, "Thank you for being

nice to me. The kids at school pick on me because I'm shorter than most of them."

"You will grow, just give it time. You'll see. You might even grow taller than all of them. What will they think then?"

Luke just smiled. He reached into his bag and pulled out a seed filled leather ball. "Do you want to play catch?"

"Sure, get over there and throw it to me." Luke was an only child, and Azan sensed he was lonely.

They played until they both grew tired.

CHAPTER 18

The second day's journey was hot and long. They found a place among the other pilgrims a considerable distance from Sukkoth, just as the sun set. Azan gazed out at the sky as the stars began to illuminate one by one.

Laying back on his bed, he thought, *God you made all of this: the heavens and the earth. I'm impressed by your amazing power. Thank you for the opportunity of taking this trip.* He closed his eyes and fell asleep.

Azan woke up and was gathering his things. They had just started out when he heard people approaching. He turned and looked back down the road. He saw a group of people, and as they got closer, Azan saw Jesus.

"Amos, it's Jesus and his friends. I'm going to go greet them." And ran off down the road.

"Jesus, I'm so glad to see you!"

"Azan, good to see you! Are you going to the Passover?"

"Yes, I am."

"Are you traveling with your family?"

"No, I've been staying with Ephraim in Capernaum for a while. My family lives in Cana. I hope to see them in Jerusalem."

"The Lord's favor be upon you!"

Andrew walked up. "Azan, I see you're coming to the Passover?"

"YES, the fishing has been slow, so Jonah let me have time to come. He was looking forward to a break from fishing."

"Well, I'm glad you can come."

They walked up to where Amos and his family was waiting, and Azan said, "This is my friend, Amos."

Jesus said, "Amos, nice to meet you."

"This is his wife, Maya, and his son Luke. They let me join them on the trip to the Passover. Ephraim couldn't make it."

"It's nice of you to allow Azan to join you and your family."

They all started down the road. Azan tried to stay as close to Jesus as possible to hear him talking to the others.

Luke was right next to him with Amos and his wife following close behind with the donkey.

He listened as Jesus said, "*As I have told you before, do not store up for yourselves treasures on earth, where moth and rust destroy and where thieves break in and steal, but store up for yourselves treasures in heaven, where neither moth nor rust destroys and where thieves do not break in and steal. For where your treasure is, there your heart will also be.*"

He taught as he walked. "*I have told you, enter by the narrow gate; for the gate is wide and broad is the way that leads to destruction, and there are many who enter through it. For the gate is narrow and the way is constricted that leads to life, and there are few who find it.*"

Jesus said, "**I have told you these things again so you will remember.**"

Azan was so mesmerized with Jesus that he did not realize how far they had traveled.

Amos called Azan over to him. "We will stop here to rest. I don't want to push my wife too much in the heat.

"Andrew, we will be stopping here to rest. I hope to see you again soon."

"Okay, have a safe journey. Good to see you."

Jesus, Andrew, and the others continued their journey. Azan wanted to stay with Jesus, but he was committed to keeping with Amos.

That night they stayed just outside of Sukkoth, staying close to other pilgrims for safety.

Amos said, "Tomorrow if we come across any

Samaritans don't speak to them. We don't want to give them a reason to come against us. Just keep walking.

They hold hostility toward the Jews. We don't need to provoke them."

The third day came, and they went around Sukkoth and were able to get through the area without conflict and continued.

I wish we could catch up with Jesus and the others. Father God, thank you for the opportunity to hear Jesus teach again. He is amazing to listen to. I hope I see him again in Jerusalem and learn more from him. Amen.

Luke came up to him. "Who is that man Jesus?"

"I believe he is the Messiah, the Holy One of God."

"I've seen him in Capernaum. People talk privately about what he has been doing. Father said, they don't want the Pharisees to hear them because they could get into trouble. I heard he healed a Centurion's servant without even being with the man."

"Yes, Jonah told me about it. He *can* heal people without being with them."

They walked all day and stayed outside Bethel the third night. While sitting around after the meal, Amos said, "I heard Jesus' teaching while we walked. It was hard to hear all of what he said with all the people around him. But I had heard that he speaks with authority. Now I see for myself. There are people in Capernaum that believe in him."

"I believe he is the Messiah."

"Be careful, the Pharisees are looking for people to make an example out of."

"I know, that's what my father is afraid of." *This is so hard. I wish the Pharisees would read the scriptures with an open mind. They would see what I see. Bethel is only an hour from here. Tomorrow we'll be in Jerusalem. I can't wait.*

∾

Azan woke up and looked into the sky. He watched as a cluster of clouds floated by. He sat up and stretched his arms above his head.

"Good morning, Amos."

"Good morning. Do you want something to eat?"

"I still have food in my bag. Thank you."

"We should be in Jerusalem by the sixth hour if we leave soon. Luke, wake up. Let's get moving."

"I'm awake." He sat up and rubbed his eyes.

They traveled on, taking breaks in the shade.

∾

"Look we're getting close; I can see the green fields and orchards in the distance."

"It won't be long now."

They reached Jerusalem and walked through the golden gate. Azan began to look through the crowds, searching for anyone who looked familiar so he might find out where his mother was staying.

Amos led them through the crowds to his brother's house in the upper city to see if they had room for them to stay.

"Amos! Hannah, my brother is here!"

Hannah came to the door, wiping her hands off on a cloth.

"Please, come in. Maya, so good to see you. Look at how tall Luke has grown. And who do we have here?"

Amos said, "This is Azan, a friend from Capernaum."

"Hello, Azan. I'm Reuben. Welcome."

"Hello, Amos has been kind enough to let me come with him and his family."

"Reuben, would you have room for us to stay while we are here? We can't stay long. Only three nights."

"Hannah and I would love to have all of you stay. It will be good to catch up with each other."

"The boys can stay in the courtyard, and you and Maya can have one of the extra rooms."

"Thank you, we will help with food and preparations for the Passover. It's a quick trip for us but it's good to see you two," Amos replied.

CHAPTER 19

E arly the following day, Azan got up and saw Amos
sitting in the courtyard.
"Good morning, Amos!"

"Good morning."

Filling up his waterskin, he said, "I'm going to look for
Mother this morning."

"I wish you well. Please be back no later than sundown so I
know you're okay."

"I will, I promise."

"Do you want to eat before you go?

"No, thank you. I will go to the market and get something."

"Okay, good luck in finding her."

"Thank you. I'll see you before dark."

*I wonder if they are staying in the same place as last year. I'll
look there first.*

He walked out into the street, and it was already teaming
with people.

*We stayed in the lower city last year. It will take a while to
walk over there. I'll go to the market first to get something to eat. I
don't think I have ever seen so many people in one place before.
There's a lot more people here than my last trip. The Roman*

soldiers are everywhere, watching for any wrong doers. I sure wouldn't want to cross them. I can smell the aromas from the marketplace. Kuddah bread sounds good, I hope they have some. It reminds me of waking up to the smell of Mothers bread. It smells so good.

He strolled through the market until he came to a booth that had a variety of breads. He walked up and searched the table for his prize.

"Do you have any Kuddah bread?"

"Over there at the end of the table."

He walked over and picked one up and said, "I'll take this one."

They exchanged the money, and he quickly turned around to walk away but ran right into a Roman soldier. The Soldier looked down at him and grabbed him tightly by the arm.

"Why don't you look where you are going? I should run you in."

Then there was a commotion about twenty-five yards away, and the soldier looked at Azan and said, "You're lucky I don't have time for you. Watch where you are going."

He shoved him as he let go of Azan's arm that was now throbbing from the tight grip, he had on him. The soldier gathered his composure and walked away toward the two who were arguing.

Whoa, that was too close. I better watch my step. I can't even think of what might have happened. Wow, I'm shaking. I need to sit for a minute.

Walking in the opposite direction of the soldier he found a tree with a little shade under it. One bite of the Kuddah bread was satisfying and he ate the whole loaf. A sip of water refreshed his mouth, and he continued his way.

"This is starting to look familiar—that's where we stabled the donkey last year. There's the place we stayed right there!"

There was a woman sitting outside grinding grain. A man came out and started talking to her.

Someone else is staying there this year. Where could they be?
He was disappointed when he did not find them there. *Did they even come this year?* Continuing to walk around he tried to hold on to hope.

He had to maneuver his way through the crowds of people. He searched the lower city and around the temple. He looked all day with no success.

It doesn't look like I'm going to find them. I don't want to go back to Capernaum before I see her. God, please let me find her.

The sun was beginning to set, and he remembered that he had promised to be back with Amos.

He was walking back with a heavy heart when he heard someone call his name.

"Azan, Azan, is that you?"

He turned around and said, "Aunt Ahava!" He ran to her, and they hugged.

"Have you seen Mother? Do you know if she is here in the city? Do you know where she might be staying?"

"Yes, your father and her are staying at my house near the Amphitheater."

"I need to see her—can you help me? I don't want to cause any trouble, but I want to see her."

"I heard what happened between you and your father. I'm so sorry that happened. Are you okay?"

"Yes, I'm okay!"

"You're here with Ephraim, right?"

"No, Ephraim couldn't make it this year. I came with a friend and his family. We're staying in the upper city. We will only be here another two nights. Can you help me see Mother? I don't think Father wants to see me. But I need to see Mother. I miss her so much."

"Your father is going to the temple tomorrow. Can you be

outside of the Amphitheatre at the tenth hour in the lower city?"

"Yes, I'll be there!"

"She misses you too! I will let her know! She will be so happy."

"Thank you, thank you so much. I'm so glad you saw me. I've been looking for her all day."

Azan had butterflies in his stomach at the possibility of seeing her. *Thank you, God, for answering my prayer. I get to see her! I get to see Mother.*

Amos was relieved to see Azan return. "Did you find your mother?"

"I ran into Ahava, my aunt. They are staying at her new house in the lower city. It is set up for me to meet with her tomorrow by the Amphitheater. My aunt is going to let my mother know that I will be there at the tenth hour. I can't wait."

With a big smile, Azan said, "Thank you for letting me come with you!"

"Of course. I'm glad you will have some time with her."

∞

Moving through the city was a challenge because of the multitudes of people. He finally arrived at the Amphitheatre and started looking in anticipation of seeing his mother.

There are too many people, I can't see around them. I'll climb up on this rock wall so I can see better. Come on, Mother, where are you? There she is!

He jumps down and pushes his way through the crowds to her. "Mother! Here I am!"

She sees him, and rushes toward him, and embraces him. She looks into his eyes and hugs him again.

"How are you? Are you okay?"

"Yes, Mother, I'm fine," he says, smiling from ear to ear.

"You have grown a bit."

"I've missed you so much! How are Heba, Todros, and Meir?"

"They're good, growing like you. They're staying with my parents while we're gone."

"How is Father?"

"He is very troubled these days. He misses you. Although he does not say it, I can tell. He has not been the same since you left. He spends a lot of time by himself, thinking and praying."

"Do you think he will ever forgive me?"

"I hope so. It may take more time. He is processing everything."

Trying to change the subject, she said, "How is Ephraim? Ahava said he isn't here with you."

"No, he was too busy in his shop and couldn't get away."

"She said that you came with a friend."

"Yes, I came with a friend and his family. Ephraim approved of it."

"Who is this friend?'

"He's one of the merchants in Capernaum. He sells fish, bread, fruit, and other things at his booth. I prefer to buy from him. He is honest, and he's a genuinely nice man. His name is Amos, his wife is Maya, and they have a son, Luke, who is eleven."

"What have you been doing in Capernaum?"

"I have a job helping an older man with his fishing business in the early mornings. I met his son on the way to Capernaum, and he took me fishing and introduced me to his father, Jonah. Jonah has taught me a lot about fishing. I spend the afternoons helping Ephraim in his shop. He's teaching me how to do blacksmithing. I enjoy being with him, but I miss home."

"I know. We all miss you. Dobah keeps asking when you're going to come home. She's a little lost without you. Your father has Todros spending a little time out with Eliah tending the sheep. He thinks he's old enough to start helping. Meir is still energetic and wants to be in the middle of everything. I'm hopeful that your father will come around and be willing to let you come home."

"Mother, I love Father, but I couldn't denounce Jesus. I have spent time with Jesus and his friends. Jonah, the fisher I work with, he has two sons, Andrew, the one I met on the road to Capernaum, and Peter. Jesus called them to follow him. I am helping their father because they are traveling so much with Jesus.

"I wish Father could see for himself who Jesus is. Then he would understand. Mother, Jesus *is* the Messiah.

The one we have been waiting for."

"I have been hearing about the miracles that Jesus is performing. It's amazing what he is doing. I don't know what to think about all of this. All I know is that your father is very troubled right now. He is trying to figure things out. Give him some more time. And pray to God that he will come around."

"I pray all the time for God to make things clear for him and for me. I want to know the truth. Jesus is teaching the truth. I passionately believe that."

"I pray that you will continue to be okay and that we will be together again soon. I can see that you have matured. I sense a peace about you. It broke my heart when your father sent you away. It helps to see that you are doing okay. I am glad that Ephraim is there for you. I cannot thank him enough. Please tell him for me."

"Does Father know that you are meeting with me?"

"Yes, I told him. He wanted to know how you are doing. Azan, he does love you. Let's pray he will come to terms with all of this. He will be back from the temple soon. I need to go before your father gets back. Please take care of yourself. It is best this way for now. I love you, Azan! I hope it will not be long before we see each other again."

"I love you too!"

They had a tough time letting go of each other. She smiled

sympathetically, with a tear in her eye as she walked away, looking back at him as she disappeared into the crowd.

He was sad that he could not go with her but thankful that he had time with her. He watched her until she was out of sight, fighting back his own tears.

∞

Azan started walking back toward the temple, watching the activity of people coming and going. He stayed as far away from the Roman soldiers as he could to avoid another encounter. He wanted to go to the temple but was afraid he might run into his father, so he walked back to the marketplace. The merchants were calling out to people as they passed to get them to buy their wares.

Azan walked around, looking at the different booths. He came to a blacksmith booth and saw a basket of nails. He picked up one of the nails and inspected it. *Ephraim makes better nails than these. His are longer and have a larger head on them.* He returned it to the basket and walked to the next booth that had apple cakes and sweet breads. *I should take something back to the house to share with Amos and his family for letting me stay with them.*

"I'll take three loaves of the sweet bread with raisins and honey and four apple cakes, please."

He found a shady spot to sit. He took out one of the apple cakes and took a bite. *Eliah loves these. He ate about a dozen at the wedding in Cana.*

He looked up and saw the Pharisees walking through the streets. People would stop and bow their heads as they passed, which was the custom.

They walk around as if they are so much better than everyone else. Jesus doesn't do that; he treats people with kindness and compassion.

They continued past Azan, and people went back to what they were doing.

Then, close to him, a group of people were talking, and he overheard them saying that the Pharisees had confronted Jesus.

Azan moved closer and heard one man say, "There was a woman caught in adultery. The law requires that she should be stoned. They asked Jesus, 'What do you say?'

"He explained that Jesus quietly stooped down and wrote on the ground. They continued to question him, so he got up and told them, **'He who is without sin among you, let him first cast a stone at her.'**

"He stooped down again and wrote on the ground. After a few minutes, He got up and all those that had brought her to him were gone. They all walked away. He asked the woman, **'Where are your accusers? Has no one condemned you?'**

"She said, 'No, not one.'

"He said to her, **'Then neither do I, go and sin no more.'**"

The man finished, "I was amazed how he responded to the Pharisees. They all just walked away."

Azan smiled. *They try to trick him, but he is wiser than them.*

I should get back to the house. I'm so glad that Amos allowed me to come with him. It was good to see Mother. He fought off more tears. *I don't know when I'll be able to see her again. It could be another year at the next Passover before I see her.*

Amos was sitting outside in front of the house and looked relieved when Azan walked up.

"I'm glad you're back. Did you see your mother?"

"Yes, I was able to spend time with her. It was good to see her but hard to let go again."

"I am glad you were able to meet with her. I imagine it *was* hard to let her go again. Is she doing well?"

"Yes, and the family is well also."

Hannah came out of the house.

"I brought two loaves of sweet bread and two apple cakes to

share with everyone." He handed them to Hannah. "I want you all to know I appreciate your kindness. Thank you."

"You're welcome. Thank you for the bread and cakes. I'm sure we will all enjoy them."

The next day was Passover, and the men had already bought a lamb and offered their sacrifice at the Temple. The morning came, and the men began to roast the lamb as the women prepared the Passover meal. Luke and Azan helped by putting tables together and arranging cushions to sit on. When they weren't busy, they played catch with Luke's ball. That night, they all enjoyed the Passover meal. Azan thought about his family and imagined them sitting together for the Passover meal. He was sad and missed celebrating with them.

∾

After the meal, Amos said, "We need to start our journey home tomorrow. We'll leave mid-morning."

That night, they sat around talking, laughing, and eating.

Luke tasted one of the apple cakes. "Wow, this is so good. I've never had one of these before."

Azan got up. "Thank you for the meal. I'm tired. I think I will go lay down."

Hannah said, "Thank you for the gift of the sweetbread and apple cakes. The apple cakes were delicious."

"You're welcome, it's the least I could do. Good night."

CHAPTER 20

A zan rolled up his bed and put his things into his bag. Luke said, "I wish we were staying longer. I like being in the big city. There is so much to see."

Azan answered, "Yes, the big city is fun, but I like living in a smaller town. People aren't in such a hurry."

They walked out of the house, and Amos said, "Thank you for taking us in. I want you to have this"—and handed him a bag of coins—"to cover any expense you had with us being here."

Reuben said, "We don't need that, keep it for yourselves. It was a pleasure to have you with us even if it was a short visit. We'll try to make a trip to visit you soon. Have a safe trip home."

Hannah hugged Maya and Luke and said, "Azan, it was nice to meet you. I'm so happy you were able to see your mother."

"Thank you for your hospitality. It was nice to meet you too."

Maya said, "Thank you again, I will look forward to you visiting us when you can."

They had the donkey loaded and started out toward the Golden Gate to leave the city. Walking through the streets they came across a Roman soldier detaining a man. The man was pleading his case and people stood around watching.

I'm glad my encounter with the Roman Soldier didn't end badly. I'm afraid to think what might have happened.

They exited the Golden Gate and started out through the green fields and orchards.

Azan looked up into the sky and watched the white billowy clouds float by.

Luke was just as talkative as he was before. Azan half listened to him as they entered the valley toward home.

Azan said, "I'll take charge of the donkey." He took the reins from Amos.

They walked six and a half hours and were on the other side of Bethel.

Amos announced, "We'll stop here for the night. Others are stopping here, and it is good to have a group of travelers around us."

The sun was setting, and the sky lit up with bright orange and pink, coloring the clouds overhead. They were sitting around after the meal and Amos said, "Azan, tell me what you know about Jesus. I'm curious to know more about him. I know he has been healing many people and teaching in the Synagogues. We've been expecting the Messiah to come in power and release us from Roman oppression. What I heard as we were walking with him seems credible. I have heard others say that he talks with authority. It is true. I've never heard anyone talk like him. Not even the Pharisees."

"I love listening to him. Jesus is full of knowledge and wisdom. I know that we have always thought that the Messiah would come and rescue us from Roman oppression. But I have heard him say that he has not come to condemn the world but to save it. Jesus loves all people, and he teaches that we are to love each other including our enemies. Jesus cares about the people, but he doesn't like their evil ways. Jesus said he has come to give life and give it abundantly. He says we are to trust in him alone."

Amos, Maya, and Luke listened.

Amos then said, "So you really believe that he is the Messiah?"

"Yes, I do. The more I hear him speak and the more I hear of all the miracles he's performing; it leaves little doubt in my mind. Who has ever done the things he has done? There has never been anyone like him."

"I would like to hear more, but it's getting late. We can talk another time."

"I would like that."

Azan rolled his bed out and laid down and prayed. *Thank you, God, for allowing me to spend time with my mother. Thank you for Amos bringing me along and the hospitality shown by his family. Thank you for the time spent with Jesus. Thank you for making a way for my father and I to come back together somehow. Amen.*

∾

Azan was awakened by a bird squawking in the tree above him. The sun was rising, and Azan opened his eyes. He heard a noise, sat up, looked up and saw Roman Soldiers on horses coming down the road. As they got closer, they started shouting for the people to get up and move along. Behind them, Samaritans were herding goats.

Amos heard the commotion and said, "Wake up, Hannah, Luke, wake up. We must move! Hurry!"

He reminded us, "Don't look at the Samaritans, and don't speak to them. Let's move away from the road while they pass. Come on, grab your things. Azan, can you take the donkey?"

Azan picked up his bed, grabbed his bag, took the reins, and started moving away from the road.

A group of pilgrims were still gathering their things when

the goats started coming through. One goat took a bag that was sitting on the ground in its mouth and was walking away with it. The man it belonged to went after the goat to retrieve the bag and was yelling at it, "Bring that back here." The goat took off running with the bag.

The Samaritans started yelling back, "Leave the goat alone! You Jews don't belong here. Get out of our land."

The Roman Soldiers turned around on their horses and came back.

"You Jews get your things and move away from the road. Let the goats go through."

The Samaritans yelled out once more, "Go back to your own land," as they passed by.

Everyone moved quickly to get their things and moved out of the way. The goats passed through, and Amos said, "Come on. Load the donkey and let's go."

We could see the goats down the road and the Samaritans herding them off the main road onto a side road, and soon they were out of sight.

After walking about an hour, Amos said, "Let's stop under those trees ahead and eat. Let's eat quickly and keep moving. The sooner we get out of Samaria, the better."

Azan took his extra head covering out of his bag and wiped his forehead and the back of his neck. There were no clouds to cast a welcome shadow, and it was getting hot. He looked off in the distance and saw stone outposts again with the soldiers standing guard.

I've had enough encounters with the Romans; let's hope we don't have any more.

They were approaching Sukkoth, and Amos said, "Let's go around Sukkoth on the outskirts to avoid any more conflict. We'll go another two miles before we stop for the night. That will put us a safe distance away from the town."

Beth Shan was the last overnight stop on the trip and

Azan was happy to be out of Samaria and closer to Capernaum.

~

Azan could feel the breeze from the Sea of Galilee as they got closer to Capernaum.

It will be good to get back to Ephraim's. I bet he is still working in the shop.

Azan was happy to be back and found Ephraim just as he thought, working in the shop as usual.

"How was the trip?" he asked.

"I saw Mother. We spent a couple of hours together talking. She said the family is doing good. She said Father hasn't been the same since I left. I wish things were different."

"Azan, I did not tell you before, but a friend of your father came by not too long ago. You were out fishing. He wanted to know how you're doing. Your father has been worried about you and asked him to inquire for him. He loves you and cares about you. You need to know that!"

"Thank you for telling me. There might be hope. Who was the friend?'

"His name was Medad. He had his son with him, Eliah I believe."

"Oh, Eliah is one of my best friends. I miss the adventures we used to have."

"They were not in town long. They came to get provisions and needed to get back to Cana.

"Medad said that your dad is questioning things, and he is troubled with the Pharisees and how they are plotting against Jesus. He does not agree with the disturbing talk he is hearing."

"What did he mean? What is disturbing him?"

"The Pharisees are talking more about getting rid of Jesus. He is threatening their authority with the Jewish people, and they will not stand for it. They are saying he must go."

"Are they talking about running him out of the area, or worse?"

"I don't know. Things are starting to heat up, and I'm not sure what will happen."

"I am glad you told me about their visit and about my father. That helps a little."

Azan went to his loft and laid on his bed. He began writing on his tablet. He wrote down what he could remember that Jesus taught on the way to Jerusalem, his visit with his mother, and the visit Ephraim had with Medad and Eliah. *God, I'm concerned for Jesus and my father. I know that father is troubled. Please help him to know the truth. Help him to know Jesus. I know you have Jesus here for a purpose. I don't know what that purpose is, but I know you are with him. Thank you again for making it possible for me to go to Jerusalem.*

Amen.

He fell asleep, exhausted from the trip.

∾

Azan rose before the sun came up and headed to the shore to find Jonah.

"Jonah, I'm back!"

"Azan, good to see you. Did you have a good trip? I can tell by the smile on your face that you saw your mother."

Jonah was a kind man and had been very patient with Azan and his lack of fishing skills. Azan tried hard to learn, and they were doing well with their catches.

Jonah told Azan, "My boys and Jesus are back in town. Jesus will be teaching in the synagogue tomorrow. I plan to go. It's the weekend, so no fishing tomorrow."

"Thank you. I will use the time to help my uncle with his work. Do you know when Jesus will be at the synagogue?"

"When he is in town, he's usually there midmorning."

After fishing and Azan telling Jonah about his trip to

Jerusalem, they came to shore, unloaded, secured the boat, and took their catch to the market.

At home, Ephraim was happy to have the help, and they talked while they worked.

Azan asked Ephraim, "Why don't you go to the synagogue?"

He replied, "I have not been since my wife died. It was too public for me, and I needed time to myself."

"Jesus is teaching tomorrow in the synagogue, and I was wondering if you would go with me?"

"The Pharisees might not welcome me after so long a time. It *would* be good to listen to Jesus and hear more of what he has to say. Yes, let's go together. The Pharisees from Jerusalem are in town. They heard Jesus has spent time here teaching and is getting more popular with the people. It might be interesting to see what happens. Yes, I'll go to town with you tomorrow."

∼

As they were approaching the synagogue, the people were exiting the building. Jesus was standing on the steps and said to them, *"You hypocrites, rightly did Isaiah prophesy of you, by saying; This people honor me with their lips, but their heart is far away from me. And in vain do they worship me, teaching as doctrines the commandments of men."*

He called to the people, and said, *"It is not what enters the mouth that defiles the person; but what comes out of the mouth, this defiles the person."*

His disciples said to him, "The Pharisees were offended after they heard this saying."

Jesus replied to them, *"Every plant, which my heavenly Father did not plant, will be rooted up. Leave them alone: they are blind guides of blind people. And if a person who is blind guides another who is blind, both will fall into a pit."*

Peter asked him, "What does this parable mean?"

"Are you also still lacking knowledge? Do you not understand that everything that goes into the mouth passes into the stomach, and is eliminated? But the things that come from the heart, and those things defile the person. For out of the heart come evil thoughts, murders, acts of adultery, other immoral sexual acts, thefts, false testimonies, and slanderous statements: These are the things that defile the person: but to eat with unwashed hands does not defile." After this, Jesus and his men left the town.

Azan saw Jonah and went up to him and asked, "What was all of that about?"

"The Pharisees confronted Jesus about his men not following the traditions of the religious leaders in washing their hands before they eat. They were trying to catch him going against their laws. He contradicted them, and it angered them. That is when the crowd started to disperse."

The Pharisees watched them walk away and said to the crowd, "There's nothing more to see here. Disperse at once."

People walked away until only the Pharisees were standing in front of the Synagogue. They were clearly upset and were talking among themselves.

Ephraim said, "Let's get back to the house."

Azan explained, "It's not about traditions. It's about the truth! They are not worried about what is right or wrong—they are just trying to catch Jesus going against their traditions."

"I am afraid that he has made enemies of the Pharisees. They will go to great lengths to stop him. He may be in danger of arrest."

"They wouldn't arrest an innocent man, would they?

Jesus hasn't done anything wrong. He is a good man, who is humble and gracious to the people. They can't name one thing he has done wrong."

"Well, he has certainly given them good reason to be concerned about who the people will follow."

∞

Azan would hear of Jesus in the areas of Tyre and Sidon, healing people. About a man who was deaf, a demon possessed girl, and multitudes of others. He heard about Jesus feeding five thousand people, and even bringing people back to life. He was convinced that Jesus was the Messiah.

CHAPTER 21

Azan continued his life in Capernaum, fishing and helping his uncle. He spent hours writing about what he heard and experienced with Jesus.

He was sitting at the table writing when Ephraim came into the house.

"Ephraim, I made lentil soup, and we have bread from the market. Are you hungry?"

"How did you know how to make lentil soup?"

"I used to stand in the kitchen and talk with mother when she was cooking. I got more out of that time with her than just our enjoyable conversation."

"I have one last thing to do on that plowshare. I won't be long. I came in to get some water."

Ephraim came in when he was done and washed his hands and face. "I think I'll get out of these smoky clothes."

"Go ahead, I'll dish up the soup."

Azan filled the two bowls with the soup and set it on the table. He sat down to wait for Ephraim. *He changes his clothes, but he still smells like smoke from the fire in his shop, just not as strong. When I smell smoke, it reminds me of him.*

Ephraim came to the table and saw Azan's writing sitting next to him.

"I see you've been writing. You must have volumes by now. Are you recording what happened at the synagogue?"

"Yes, I like to write as soon as I can, while it is still fresh in my mind. I wouldn't be able to remember everything if I didn't write it down. It also helps me to use what I have learned in school."

Ephraim prayed over the meal, tore a piece of bread off and dipped it into the soup.

"This soup tastes good. By now you know I don't enjoy cooking, so thank you for making this. Can you read me something from your writings?"

"Okay. Let me see. Did I tell you about the ruler who came to Jesus and told him his daughter had died?"

"No, I don't remember that."

"Jesus was in Gadarenes and a ruler came to him, worshiped him, and said that his daughter had died. He told Jesus, 'my daughter has died, but come and lay your hand on her and she will live.'

"When Jesus went to the house, there were people there wailing. Jesus said to them, '**Make room, for the girl is not dead, but sleeping.**' The people ridiculed him. So, he had them put outside.

"He went into the girl and took her by the hand, and the girl arose. He raised her from the dead. The people were amazed, and they spread the news of this in all the land. That's how I heard about it."

"I've never heard of anyone being raised from the dead."

"There are so many that he has healed. It's amazing.

I'm so thankful I am here to experience these things. Knowing him has changed how I think. How I want to live. It has changed the course of my life."

"It certainly did change the course of your life. You are here in Capernaum, aren't you? You have grown in stature since you've been here. But you have also grown spiritually. You are wiser than most boys your age."

"The Pharisees are so worried about him. He has power over them, and they know it. They are only out for themselves. If they only knew what they are doing."

"He is the Messiah. Who else can do all these things?"

Azan got the biggest smile on his face. He had someone who could share in the experience of knowing who Jesus is.

Ephraim seems more at peace with his life since he became a believer.

∽

As time went on, Amos and his family became close friends, and Azan began to tolerate Luke and a friendship was formed. Ephraim and Azan would get together with them for meals, and on one occasion, Eliana, Amos' sister was there, and he introduced them. *She is pretty. I didn't know Amos had a sister. She's as tall as Amos but she has a slim build. She has long straight light brown hair with eyes to match.*

"Eliana, this is Azan and his uncle Ephraim. He has a blacksmith shop near here."

"It's nice to meet you, Azan and Ephraim."

Ephraim said, "Nice to meet you also. Are you from around here?"

"No, I live with my parents in Chorazin north of here."

They sat down next to each other and began talking.

It would be nice if Ephraim made some friends to encourage him to be out more. He looks like he is enjoying himself. This is good for him. I have hope that he will start living again.

It ended up that they spent the rest of the day together talking and enjoying each other's company.

On the way home, Azan said, "It looks like you enjoyed Eliana's company today."

"Yes, I did."

"She seems really nice." Ephraim just smiled.

∾

Jesus and his disciples happened into Capernaum after a long absence. They had been touring the country north of Capernaum for a month. Jonah had Azan over to see Andrew and Peter while they were in town.

When he arrived at the house, Andrew came out and greeted him. "Azan, I hear you are becoming quite the fisher. My father said you have come a long way. Thank you for helping him. He's getting older, and it comforts me to know that you are here."

"Thank you, I am getting the hang of it.

Where have you all been? I have been hearing reports of the healing that Jesus has been doing."

"Good news travels fast. We went north to Caesarea Philippi, Mt. Herman, and east to Tyre and Sidon.

The word is spreading about Jesus. More people are believing."

"I have seen it here in Capernaum also. My uncle is now a believer. It has changed his life and mine also."

"That is why Jesus is here, to change people's lives. I never know how long we will be here. We will be in town tomorrow if you want to come and listen to him teach."

"It's the weekend, I would love to come. I'll bring Ephraim."

They invited Azan to eat with them.

PETER SAID, "Jesus has been doing amazing things. Father, did you tell Azan how Jesus healed Mother? She was ill, and my wife was caring for her in our home. It was difficult for her with Andrew and I being away so much. Jesus went to her, prayed over her, touched her, and healed her. Mother jumped up and started moving around the house waiting on us. Now, I don't have to worry about what is going on at home."

They visited for a couple of hours, and Peter said he needed to get back to his house.

Azan excused himself and went home.

∞

In town the next day, it was busy with people and a crowd was gathering at the end of the market square.

Jesus was there with his disciples.

Azan and Ephraim stood as close as they could get to Jesus.

He said, *"The Pharisees asked when the kingdom of God was coming, and I said to them, the kingdom of God is not coming with signs that can be observed; nor will they say, look here it is, or there it is! For behold, the kingdom of God is in your midst."*

The disciples asked him, "Who is the greatest in the kingdom of heaven?"

Then Jesus called a little *child* to him and set him amid them. *"Truly I say to you. Except you be converted, and become as little children, you will not enter the kingdom of heaven. Whosoever will humble himself as a little child, the same is greatest in the kingdom of heaven. And whosoever will receive one such little child in my name receives me."*

They sat and listened to Jesus through the afternoon.

At home that night, Azan thought about what Jesus said. *To be considered a child of God, you must be humble as a little child. Am I being humble? What is in my heart? Am I honoring God with my life? I know that I have sinned. God help me to honor you and be humble before you.*

∞

Jesus and the twelve disciples left Capernaum after a couple of days.

Azan continued to hear that the Pharisees were plotting to arrest Jesus for blasphemy. He asked himself, *why can't they understand who Jesus is? They are supposed to be the leaders who teach God's word. Have they become so interested in their own influence that it has blinded them?*

CHAPTER 22

Between fishing and the shop, Azan kept busy. During his alone time, he continued to write down everything he heard about Jesus, all the reports of healing and his teachings, and the plot of the Pharisees. *I want to capture everything I can, concerning Jesus. It gives me hope, and I want to share it with Father at some point. It might help him to understand that Jesus is the Messiah.*

...

Azan was sitting at the table writing when Ephraim came in and announced, "I have arranged to visit Eliana. Your skills have increased, and I have confidence in your work. If you don't mind, I have certain projects for you to work on while I am away."

"I'm glad to help. What project do you want me to work on?"

"We have an order for twenty-four horseshoes. You can start there. That will keep you busy for a while."

"Okay, you really like Eliana, don't you?"

"I enjoy her company. I will be meeting her family today.

Wish me success with her father. I hear he is very protective of her."

"You're a good man. I'm sure he will approve."

"I guess I will find out. I must admit I'm a little nervous. I will be back by sundown."

"Okay, have a good visit with her and her parents."

Ephraim went into the house and when he came out, his hair was combed, and he had on his best clothes. He smelled of cassia which diminished the smell of smoke.

Azan just smiled. "See you tonight!"

Ephraim nervously smiled back as he walked away.

∾

Azan went off to join Jonah for a morning of fishing. "Good morning, Jonah. Looks like we have mild weather today."

"There you are. I got here early to repair the net. I just finished. Help me get it into the boat."

They talked as they rowed out a distance. "Any word from Peter and Andrew?"

"Not really. I did hear they were in upper Galilee. I'm not sure when they will be back in Capernaum. "

"I hope they return soon. I love hearing about the things Jesus has been doing. I want to spend more time with him. I just worry about his safety. There has been more talk about the Pharisees and their desires to get rid of him."

"Yes, he is threatening the Pharisees with his popularity. More people are following and believing in him."

After they returned and went to the market with their catch, Azan went back and started working in the shop.

The coals are still hot from last night. He grabbed some wood and threw it into the coals. *Let's see, this is the last one Ephraim made.* He looked at it, took a metal rod, and set the end of it in the fire that was now blazing. *I can get three or four of them done before Ephraim gets back. I hope things go well for him and Eliana. It would be great to see them get together. I think he would be happy with her.*

Later, Ephraim came walking up to the house and saw Azan working in the shop. Azan looked up and said, "Hey, Ephraim, you're back. How is Eliana?"

He smiled. "She's doing good. How's the project going?"

"I thought I could get four of them done before you returned, but I only completed three. It took longer than I thought it would."

"Oh, I am glad you got the three done. That is tedious work, and it takes time. Thank you!"

"Sure."

"So, how did it go with Eliana's family?"

"It looks like things went well. They were hospitable and tried to make me feel welcomed."

"That's great. I'm glad it went well—you seem happier these days."

"I am. We enjoy each other's company. It's nice. I didn't realize how lonely I was until you came to stay with me. You helped me be more open to the possibilities."

∾

Jonah was waiting for him the next day. He had everything ready to go. They shoved off and rowed out about a mile. They dropped the nets and sat back to wait for the catch.

Azan noticed that something was bothering Jonah. "Is something wrong? Did I get here late? Did I do something to upset you?"

"No, you're okay. I am worried that things might be getting worse for Jesus. Peter got word to me through his wife. Jesus told them that all things written through the prophets about the Son of Man will be fulfilled. That he will be handed over and mistreated. He said they will scourge him and kill him.

Then Jesus said something strange. That on the third day he will rise again."

"Why did he say these things? He is the Messiah! No, it can't be! We finally have the Messiah and now He must die?"

"I know this is hard to hear. But I trust Peter, and I know he would not pass that along if Jesus had not said it." Azan did not want to believe that this could happen. He was quiet for most of the day. Jonah didn't talk much either.

Azan was trying to go over in his mind what he had read in the Scripture about the Messiah. "Jonah, can you help me recall Isaiah? It was in Chapter 53, where it said, '*He was despised and rejected by men, a man of sorrows and acquainted with grief. Like one from whom men hide their faces, he was despised, and we esteemed him not.*'"

"Yes, it says, '*Surely, he took up our pain and bore our suffering, yet we did consider him punished by God, stricken by him, and afflicted. But he was pierced for our transgressions, he was crushed for our iniquities: the punishment that brought us peace was on him, and by his wounds we are healed.*'"

Azan continued, "'*We all, like sheep have gone astray, each of us has turned to his own way; and the Lord has laid on him the iniquity of us all.*'

'*He was oppressed and afflicted, yet he did not open his mouth; he was led like a lamb to the slaughter, and a sheep before its shearers is silent, so he did not open his mouth.*'"

Then these words came to Azan. "Behold the Lamb of God who takes away the sin of the world. He is the *lamb*!"

They looked at each other and thought about these things. Azan became more troubled about what might happen to Jesus.

He thought, *Jesus is an innocent man who has done nothing but help people. He heals the blind, but the Pharisees are blind even though they can see. How can they condemn an innocent man to death? Don't they have a heart for what is good and pleasing?*

They are so caught up in maintaining their way of life that they are willing to go to great lengths to keep it secure.

That night, Azan wrote all these things and pondered them. Jesus knows what is going to happen. But if he wanted to stop it, he could.

CHAPTER 23

The next year flew by, and Azan had grown to be as tall as Ephraim. With all the physical work he had been doing, he had developed a strong build. But the most striking thing was his boldness to proclaim Jesus. Anyone who would listen to him would get a full sense of who Jesus was.

Azan could not believe it had been a year since he had met with his mother in Jerusalem. He realized that the next Passover Feast was fast approaching.

He was in town on Saturday, talking with people he knew and interacting with the children. He enjoyed their company but still missed Dobah, Todros, and Meir.

Luke came running up to him out of breath, saying, "Jesus and his disciples are coming into town. Let's go meet them."

"I'll beat you there!"

Azan took off running with Luke close behind, and they came to where they could see the group walking in the distance.

Azan was excited to see them after such a long time.

As they got closer, Andrew shouted, "Azan! Look how you've grown. You look strong and healthy. How's Father doing? How is the fishing?"

"Jonah is doing good! Still determined!"

Peter laughed. "That sounds about right!"

Jesus said, *"That's what keeps him going. How are you? The last time we spoke, you were hoping to see your mother."*

"I did see her, but it's been almost a year already."

"Yes, time has passed and we're just about at Passover again."

"Are you staying in town long?"

"We'll be here for a while. You should join us while we're here."

"Yes, I will, thank you."

The boys walked with them into town and people started crowding around Jesus, so Azan said, "Let's meet up with

Jesus and the others later." They said their goodbyes to

Andrew and went on their way.

Azan found them the next day by the shore. Jesus was sitting talking to a group of people. Azan sat down to listen.

Jesus said, **"I am the good shepherd: the good shepherd lays down his life for the sheep. He who is a hired hand, and not a shepherd, who is not the owner of the sheep, sees the wolf coming, and leaves the sheep and flees; and the wolf snatches them and scatters the flock. He flees because he is a hired hand and does not care about the sheep. I am the good shepherd; and I know My own sheep and my own know Me. Just as the Father knows Me and I know the Father; and I lay down My life for the sheep. And I have other sheep that are not of this fold; I must bring them also, and they will listen to My voice, and they will become one flock and with one shepherd.**

The reason My Father loves Me, is that I lay down My life so I may take it back. No one has taken it from Me, but I lay it down on My own. I have authority to lay it down, and I have the authority to take it back. This command

I have received of my Father."

The people listening said, "He has a demon, and he is raving mad. Why listen to him?"

Others said, "These are not the sayings of a man possessed by a demon. Can a demon open the eyes of the blind?"

On hearing this, Azan remembered what he had heard in town about how Jesus healed a man blind from birth in Bethsaida. The Pharisees were trying to dispute that the man was blind to begin with, but the man affirmed that he was blind from birth and now he sees. They had even questioned his parents to see if he truly was blind from birth. The man was blind and now he sees.

∞

After spending time listening to Jesus, Azan had to get back to his responsibilities.

Later that night, Azan laid on his bed thinking. This was another account that he added to the list of things he had written down. He often read back on his entries and marveled at all that Jesus had done. *I know this is just a small amount of the miracles and teachings of Jesus. But it gives me great peace knowing who Jesus is.*

∞

The Passover was just a month away, and people started talking about making the yearly pilgrimage to Jerusalem.

"Ephraim, I wish you would come with me to the Passover this year. We can both work to get ahead of the projects."

"I've been thinking about it, and I think I *will* go this year. We could travel with Amos and his family. I prefer to travel in numbers, especially after what happened on your return trip through Samaria last time."

"I'm sure Amos would agree. I will ask him tomorrow when I see him."

After the morning fishing trip, Azan took the catch to Amos and made the transaction.

"Amos, are you going to Passover again this year? Ephraim and I are going, and he said he would like to travel with you and your family if you plan to go. He says there is safety in numbers."

"Oh, that would be good. Yes, we are going, tell Ephraim we would be pleased to travel with you two. We'll be staying with my brother Reuben and his wife Hannah again this year. I know they will welcome you."

While in town, he searched around to see where Jesus and the disciples were. He found them at the olive grove where the usually stay when in town.

"Jesus, good to see you. It looks like you are preparing to leave again. Where are you going this time?"

"We will be going towards Jerusalem with some stops along the way. Will you be going to Passover again this year?"

"Yes, Ephraim and I will be making the trip with Amos and his family."

"That's good. I'm glad Ephraim is coming with you this year. I imagine you are hoping to see your mother again. Family is important, I'm sure there is a good possibility for you to see her and others from your family."

"Yes, I do hope for that. It's been a long time."

Then Jesus said, **"There will be trouble in this life, but it works for your good if you believe!"**

What did he mean by that? How can something difficult turn out to be good for you? Sometimes it is hard to understand what he is saying. Should I ask him?

Jesus started talking to the others, and Azan didn't get a chance to ask him what he meant.

Jesus and his disciples started preparing for their trip towards Jerusalem, although Passover was still three weeks away.

Azan was talking with Andrew, and he said, "We're stopping in Bethany, to visit Mary, Martha, and Lazarus the friends of Jesus. We are also planning on spending time in Judea before entering Jerusalem. We hope to see you there."

"Should Jesus even be going into Jerusalem? It could be dangerous for him to go there."

"That's what we keep telling him, but he is determined to go."

∞

After they left, Azan remembered, *Lazarus was the man from Bethany that Jesus had raised from the dead. His sisters had sent for Jesus because Lazarus was sick. But, by the time Jesus got to Bethany, the man had died. They said he had been in the tomb for four days. Jesus went to the tomb and had the stone rolled away, then in a loud voice he had said,* **"Lazarus, come forth!"** *And Lazarus came out still wrapped in the graveclothes. Jesus said to loosen him and let him go. Many people that saw it, believed in him. But others went to the Pharisees and told them what they had seen. I know Jesus is in danger going into Jerusalem. I remember what he said that the shepherd gives his life for his sheep.*

It kept ringing in his ears. He still wondered what Jesus meant when he said he has the authority to lay it down, and the authority to take it up again.

His saying are hard to understand at times.

∞

The days passed quickly, and it was time to start the journey to Jerusalem.

Ephraim and Azan had bought bread, fruit, and dried fish

from the market and packed it for the trip. They filled up their water skins and rolled up their sleeping mats. Azan was happy that Ephraim was going with him.

Amos and his family met them on the road that passed by Ephraim's house. They had Eliana with them.

Ephraim went up to her and said, "Good morning, Eliana. I didn't know you were coming with Amos. I'm happy to see that you're joining us."

"Good morning, Ephraim. My aunt Hannah, in Jerusalem, sent word requesting me to come. We just got the message the day before yesterday. I'm happy to be going. It has been a while since I have seen her and her family. My father was comfortable with me coming with my brother Amos."

Azan looked at Ephraim, who had the biggest smile on his face, went over to Luke and said, "Let's get this caravan moving."

They started off, and Luke began talking as usual. This time Azan joined in on the conversations. They had become friends, and Azan enjoyed his friendship.

CHAPTER 24

The group set off early in the morning toward Jerusalem.

They arrived safely in Jerusalem a week before Passover and went to Amos' brother's house. Hannah was outside grinding grain in the shade of the porch. She looked up when she heard her name.

"Hannah!"

"Maya! I was hoping that you would be coming to Passover!"

She called out to Reuben, "Amos and the family are here from

Capernaum."

Reuben came to the door. "Welcome, come in!"

Amos said, "I hope we aren't being too presumptuous in thinking we could stay here again."

Hannah said, "Of course, you can stay. Eliana, so good to see you, I'm glad your father agreed to let you come. And who is this with you?"

Eliana explained. "You know Azan, and this is Azan's uncle, Ephraim. He owns a blacksmith shop in Capernaum."

"It's nice to meet you, Ephraim. Azan is a wonderful boy. He was delightful last year when he stayed with us. Welcome to our home."

"Thank you, it's nice to meet you. Azan and Amos have told me about you."

"I hope it was all good." Laughing, she turned to Azan and Luke. "Look at the two of you. You have both grown so much since
last year."

Hannah said, "Eliana, you can stay in this room here. Amos and Maya, you can stay in that one there.

We can make you three comfortable out here in the courtyard. You'll get a cool breeze through the night. And there's plenty of stars to look at through the opening. There should be plenty of room for the three of you. Go ahead set your things down."

Ephraim said, "We are thankful for a place to stay. The courtyard is perfect."

Azan, Ephraim, and Luke took their things and set them in a corner of the courtyard.

Luke said, "It'll be fun to sleep in the courtyard so we can watch for more shooting stars."

The women made a meal, and they all sat around laughing and talking till dark.

Reuben said, "There is a lot of anticipation about Jesus coming to Jerusalem. People are talking about Jesus healing a blind man in Jericho. The people were astonished when they heard he had raised a man from his grave. All they can talk about is Jesus and all the miracles he has performed. People are wondering if he is coming to Passover. Everyone, except the Pharisees and authorities, are anxiously waiting to see him here."

"Jesus *is* coming. He and his followers were headed this way. I saw them in Capernaum before they started their journey."

~

Azan and Ephraim spent time the next day walking around Jerusalem, taking in all the sights, sounds, and the aromas. Ephraim had not been to the Passover since the year before his wife's death. He said, "I thought there were a lot of people here the last time I came, but I am amazed at the number of people that are here now."

Azan said, "I wonder if Father and Mother are here this year?

I would love to see them. I would like to talk to my father, but

I am not sure he wants to talk to me."

"I can search for them and talk to your father, to see if he is willing to meet with you. I think it has been long enough. I hope we can get resolution to his opposition. I will keep my eyes and ears open for them."

"Thank you, I hope we can find them. Do you want to go to the temple?"

"Yes, I would like to see it again."

Once inside the temple grounds, they could see the

Pharisees and the scribes walking through the crowds. People would bow their heads as they walked by. The money changers sat at their tables with lines of people waiting. People had lambs on their shoulders and others had goats and rams leading them through the crowds. Passover was not until the end of the week, so they decided to wait to buy a lamb for their Passover meal.

They left the temple and went towards the golden gate. They saw crowds of people gathering and shouting. They had palm branches and were laying their cloaks on the road. Then Azan saw Jesus, riding on a young donkey. People were shouting, "Hosanna! Blessed is he who comes in the name of the Lord! Blessed is the coming kingdom of our father David!"

Jesus rode the donkey through the streets filled with people clamoring to see Him. Azan and Ephraim followed the procession to the temple. Jesus went in and looked around at everything and started yelling at the money changers and knocking over their tables.

Azan told Ephraim, "This is the second time I have seen him doing this. He doesn't like them selling inside the temple."

People started scattering away from him. He left the temple with the twelve disciples and headed out of the city.

Azan and Ephraim watched them as they made their way out of the courtyard and out of their sight.

Azan was thrilled to see the people worshiping Jesus. But he was genuinely concerned about the scribes and the Pharisees and what they might do to Him.

He saw them watching Jesus and talking to each other.

Azan said to Ephraim, "I hope the Pharisees do not do something during Passover to Jesus. People are believing who he is, and I don't think they like the attention he is getting."

"You're right they don't like it at all. It takes attention away from their power and authority. They want to keep the people in line with their laws and traditions. They just don't know who they are dealing with."

∾

Azan said, "Let's go to the marketplace. I want to get something to take back to the house to share with the family." He led Ephraim through the street to the booth that he had visited before.

"You must try this Kuddah bread. It is good, but the best I've ever tasted is Mother's Kuddah bread." Azan bought four loaves. He broke off a piece of one and handed it to Ephraim. "Try it. You'll love it."

Ephraim smelled it and took a bite. "Mm this *is* good."

They spent the day walking around the city, enjoying all the sights. Azan was looking through the crowds thinking, *if only I could find out where Mother might be staying.* Then he heard, "Azan! Azan!"

He turned around and there was Eliah, Medad, and Galia.

"Eliah! I'm so glad to see you."

Ephraim said, "Medad, good to see you again."

"Ephraim this is my wife, Galia. Galia, this is Azan's uncle, Ephraim."

"I'm glad you are here. How long are you going to be in Jerusalem?"

"We will be here a week or two."

"Have you seen my mother and father?"

"Yes, we came with them, and we're all staying with your Aunt Ahava in the lower city.

"Your parents and your brothers and your sister are here."

"All of them are here? I want to see them! Can you let them know that we are staying in the upper city at a friend's house?"

"They are hoping to see you here. I will tell them you're here with Ephraim."

Ephraim said, "I'll go to Ahava's house tomorrow and talk to them."

"Azan, Let's get together while we're here. Father, would that be okay with you?" Eliah asked.

Medad replied, "Yes, I'm sure you two have a lot of catching up to do."

"Can we meet tomorrow, right here? This is about halfway between the upper and lower cities."

"Okay—about the sixth hour?"

"Okay, I'll see you tomorrow."

"Do you know how long my family will be here?"

"They have plans to stay here for a week or two after Passover."

"I sure hope I can see them."

Ephraim said, "I'm sure we can arrange something. I plan to talk to your father while I'm there to see if he is willing to meet with you."

"Thank you. I hope so."

"We'll see what happens."

∽

The next morning, Ephraim announced, "I'm going to go to Ahava's house. I'll be back by sundown."

Azan said, "Tell them I'm looking forward to seeing them." *I hope Ephraim can talk Father into meeting with me. I don't know how it will turn out, but I must try. God, I pray that you will reunite me with my family. It's been a long time.*

"I'm going to go meet with Eliah. I will be spending the day with him."

"Okay, I'll meet you back here tonight. I'll let you know how the meeting went."

∽

Azan returned to where Eliah had agreed to meet. He looked around but didn't see him at first. Then he saw Eliah sitting in the shade of a building.

"Eliah, there you are."

"Azan, I sure have missed you. It's lonely watching the sheep by myself. Todros comes out occasionally, but it's different than it was with you. I brought some food, come, and sit down."

"How are things at home?"

"Not much has changed. Do you know when you will be coming back?"

"I'm hoping that I can talk to my father while I'm here. I don't know if he is even willing to talk to me. I guess he's still mad at me."

"What happened between you two? My father won't say too much about it. I just know that your interest in Jesus caused a division between you two. I tried to warn you."

"Yes, you did. He was so angry, he wanted me to denounce

Jesus. I just couldn't. Eliah, He *is* the Messiah. I honestly believe it. I've spent time with him and his men in

Capernaum. He's the one we've been waiting for."

"You have been with him?"

"Yes, on more than one occasion. He is remarkable. I have no doubt that *he is* the Messiah."

"We have heard so much about him in Cana. Some people believe and others don't. There is a division in town, and the Pharisees have warned people not to discuss it, but everyone is talking about him behind closed doors."

"What do *you* think about Jesus?"

"Father and I have talked about it. No one has ever done the things Jesus has done. I think he *could* be the Messiah; I just don't know enough to make a good decision."

"I wish you could see what I have seen and heard from him. Why else would the Pharisees be so concerned about him? He is threatening them and their position among the people. He has power over them, and they know it."

The boys spent the day roaming around and talking about school, fishing, sheep tending, and blacksmithing.

∾

Later that day, when Azan returned to Reuben's house, he was waiting impatiently for Ephraim to return. Finally, he arrived back at the house. Azan ran out to meet him and excitedly said, "Did you talk to Mother? Is she able to meet with me? How are my brothers and my sister?"

Ephraim said, "Slow down, Azan. I talked to them, and your mother is happy to meet with you. She will bring Dobah, Todros, and Meir with her over here on Friday at the sixth hour. They will come here to visit."

"What about Father? Is he willing to come?"

"He was not there. Your mother said he had business with

the Pharisees. She was not sure if he would come or not. But she would ask him."

Azan went with the men the next day to the temple to buy the lamb for Passover, which was just two days away. As they walked, he thought to himself. *I remember what Father told me on my first trip to Jerusalem. He said that the lamb stood for the time when the Israelites where captive in Egypt and they were to take a lamb without blemish and kill it at twilight. And to take its blood and put it on the two doorposts and on the lintel on the house where they eat it.*

And he remembered him say, "It is the Lord's Passover."

He remembered how the firstborn of the Israelites survived when the angel of death passed over them. But those of the Egyptians' perished because of God's judgement in Egypt. The blood of the lamb protected the Israelites.

CHAPTER 25

Azan laid awake that night thinking and praying, mostly about having a chance to speak with his father. *I want to repair our relationship. I remember Father telling me how proud he was of me after my Bar Mitzvah. I remember telling him that I would follow all the laws and traditions of our Jewish religion.*

Then I met Jesus, and it all changed. I'm fifteen years old now. I have changed in a lot of ways. Being away from my family and working has caused me to be independent and responsible for myself and my actions. But knowing Jesus has changed me the most. God, please make it possible to meet with father and be able to resolve our differences. More than anything else, help father know that Jesus is the Messiah, the Christ.

∾

Azan woke up to Ephraim shaking his shoulder. "Azan, wake up!"

"What, is something wrong?"

"Yes, they have arrested Jesus! They led him off to Caiaphas the High Priest."

Azan was still waking up when he realized what he was hearing. "They arrested him. Oh, no! What charge did they bring against him?"

"They are claiming blasphemy. Because he claims to be from God. Because he claims to be the Christ. They handed him over to Caiaphas."

Azan got up and told Ephraim, "I must go. I must see this for myself. He has done nothing wrong. I can't believe they would arrest an innocent man."

"I'll come with you." As they ran through the streets, they heard they had moved Jesus to Pilates' court. They arrived and stood outside with crowds of people. Pilate, the Roman Governor of Judea, came out, stood before the people, and said, "What accusation do you bring against this man?"

The chief priest and rulers answered and said to him, "If he were not an evildoer, we would not have delivered him to you."

"You take him and judge him according to your law."

"It is not lawful for us to put anyone to death."

Pilate went inside, and when he returned, he said, "I have spoken to this Jesus, and I find no fault in him at all. Neither I nor Herod the Jewish Governor of the region, have found anything deserving of death. So, I will chastise him and release him."

But they all cried out, "Away with this man, release Barabbas."

"You have a custom that I release someone to you at the Passover. Do you want me to release to you the King of the Jews?"

Again, the crowd cried out, "Away with this man, release Barabbas!"

Azan asked a man next to him, "Who is Barabbas?"

The man said, "He is a notorious prisoner."

Pilot, wanting to release Jesus, again called out to them, but they shouted, "Crucify him! Crucify him!"

He tried once more, but they were insistent, and with loud

voices, cried out for him to be crucified. He then released Barabbas and delivered Jesus into the hands of the soldiers.

They brought him out and led Jesus off to be scourged.

Azan was horrified. They pushed their way through the crowds and followed them.

They tied him to a post, and one of the soldiers took a whip.

Azan looked at the whip. "Ephraim, look. The whip has sharp bones intertwined in it."

The soldier took the whip by the handle and threw the length of it behind him. He pulled it forward with as much strength as he had, and it landed in Jesus' back.

The soldier whipped it back away from Jesus and it tore his skin as Jesus cried out in agony.

Azan felt sick to his stomach at the sight of blood gushing from his wound. Each of the prescribed thirty-nine strikes caused deep wounds. His blood flowed down his body and puddled at his feet. When the soldier finally stopped, Jesus was unrecognizable.

Azan held on to Ephraim's arm to steady himself. Jesus became so weak from the torture that he was struggling to stand.

He watched as the soldiers took him inside, and when they brought him out again, they had made a crown of thorns and placed it on him. The thorns were imbedded into his head and blood streamed down his face. The soldiers mocked him and spit into his face. They took him down the stairs and made him carry the cross they planned to hang him on.

Azan began sobbing uncontrollably. "I can't believe what they are doing to him. Look, he can hardly stand; he's struggling under the weight of it."

He tried to take a step and fell on his knees with the weight of the cross crushing down on him.

Oh Jesus, I'm so sorry. I wish I could help you.

Then a soldier walked over to a man in the crowd and ordered him to carry the cross. He tried to say no, but they grabbed him and pushed him to the cross, yelling at him to pick it up. They followed the procession through the streets. At one point, Jesus fell to his knees, and a woman from the crowd came and wiped his face with a cloth. Azan saw the look on his face. He looked at the woman as if she were the one suffering. He had such compassion in his eyes for her.

Azan and Ephraim followed them out of the city. People were shouting at him, and others were weeping. Azan was shaking from the shock of what was playing out in front of him. They took him to a place named Golgotha outside the city. The man lowered the cross to the ground. Then they laid Jesus across it.

Azan and Ephraim watched from a short distance. Then they stretched Jesus' arms out. One held him down while another soldier had a spiked nail and a hammer and placed the nail in one of Jesus' hands. Then he heard Jesus cry out in pain, and Azan gasped. The sound of metal hitting metal was deafening. Azan went to his knees and cupped his head in his hands and screamed, "No!"

The next thing he remembered was Ephraim sitting with him on the ground, holding him and slapping his cheek.

Azan came to his senses and said, "This must be a nightmare. This can't be happening."

Ephraim tried to comfort him and got him up and moved him back away from where they were.

Ephraim helped him to the ground and sat with his arm around him. They watched as the soldiers lifted the cross and put it in the hole to stand it up. They dropped it into the hole, and it violently jarred Jesus as it hit the bottom. Jesus wrenched in pain.

One of the soldiers offered him something to drink, but he refused it.

As Azan sat there looking up at Jesus, the sky became dark with clouds.

Crying uncontrollably, he said, "I can't bear this!" Ephraim tried to comfort him, but he was inconsolable. He buried his face in his hands and began to pray.

Then he felt someone grab him under his arms and start pulling him up. He turned around, and it was his father, Yosef. He looked at his father and saw that he was sobbing also. They embraced each other for a long time. They sat down on the ground, and Yosef wrapped his arm around Azan.

Azan kept looking at him in disbelief. He couldn't say a word. They sat in silence and watched the soldiers' cast lots for Jesus' clothes. People were walking by the cross, mocking him. He heard Jesus say, ***"Forgive them, Father, for they know not what they do."***

Yosef looked at Ephraim. "We went to where you are staying, and they told me where you went. I came looking for you."

They sat there together until Jesus took his last breath. Just then an earthquake struck and shook the ground, and the people became frightened and started leaving the area.

Then a soldier came and broke the legs of the thief to the left of Jesus and then the one on the right of him. He went and stood in front of Jesus and noticed he was already dead and didn't break his legs. He took his spear and pierced it into Jesus' side, and a gush of blood and water flowed out.

They watched as some men came with ladders. They took him down as gently as they could. They wrapped him in grave clothes. They all stood up and watched as they carried his lifeless body past them.

Azan, wiping tears from his face, said, "Did you see what they wrote and placed above his head on the cross?"

Yosef replied, "Jesus of Nazareth, the King of the Jews."

"He was the King of the Jews, and they killed him."

Yosef and Ephraim took each side of Azan and led him away. They took him back to Reuben's house and told the family that Jesus was dead. They were all in shock, and the women cried. Azan was so exhausted from his emotions that they laid him on his bed, and he cried himself asleep.

∾

The morning came, and Azan got up, but he was in a daze. *Did that really happen? How are we to go on without Jesus?*

Yosef was sitting at the table, and when he saw Azan, he got up walked over to him and hugged him. Azan didn't know how to respond, other than to hug him back.

Yosef said, "Come walk with me. We need to talk." Azan looked at him and followed him to a quiet place. They sat down and Yosef said to him, "I want you to know that I love you. I now know that you were right the whole time about Jesus. I was under the traditions of men and wanted to keep my status with the Pharisees. I could not see what you saw." Azan looked at his father and tears flowed down his face. Yosef pulled him close. "I was so torn about demanding that you leave the house that I started questioning things.

"One thing you asked me was, 'How can we know if Jesus was the Messiah unless we investigate it?' I remembered the scripture that Jesus read in the synagogue in Nazareth and went and studied it, just like you did. Then I remembered that you had heard that he was born in Bethlehem. I made a trip to Nazareth and visited Mary, his mother. She confirmed that he was born in Bethlehem. She said that his birth was recorded as part of the census. You said, 'If he is the Son of God, wouldn't it be worse for us if we denied him?'"

Azan's eyes grew big at what he was hearing. "Are you saying that you believe Jesus is the Messiah?"

"Let me continue. I watched as the Pharisees and Scribes and the Sadducees were plotting to kill him. I could not agree with them that an innocent man should die. Nothing that he was doing would call for a death sentence. He had done nothing wrong.

"I came to Jerusalem to see what they were saying concerning Jesus and was in the presence of the Pharisees and the high priests yesterday. They were talking about how to arrest and kill Jesus. One member of the Pharisees reminded them that their law requires that a person charged with a crime must be heard before being judged. They ignored what he said and continued to plot against Jesus.

"You also asked, 'Unless we hear what he has to say and compare it with scripture, how can we know if he is the Messiah or not?'

"When I was here in Jerusalem last year, Jesus was teaching, and I heard him for the first time. He said, '*The scribes and the Pharisees sit in Moses' seat. Therefore, they tell you what to observe, but do not do according to their works; for they say, and do not do. He said that they love the best places at feasts, the best seats in the synagogues, greetings in the marketplaces and to be called 'Rabbi, Rabbi.'*

"Jesus helped me realize that they are selfish religious officials who take advantage of others. Yes, Azan, Jesus is the Messiah. I believe."

Azan was overjoyed to hear these words and embraced his father. "I am sorry I disrespected you. I promised to follow the law and the traditions, and I went against you."

"Azan, I told you that you were young and that you had much to learn. I was the babe who needed to learn. You are wise beyond your years. Can you please forgive *me*?"

"I have been praying for so long. Yes, of course, I forgive you. Can you forgive *me*?"

"There is nothing to forgive. You followed your heart and for that, I am proud of you."

CHAPTER 26

When they returned to the house, Heba, Dobah, Todros, and Meir were waiting for them. Azan ran to his mother and hugged her tight.

Then he turned to Meir. "Look how big you are! Todros, you are as tall as Dobah." He held out his arms, and they all came running to him and they embraced each other. Ephraim and Eliana were standing in the doorway with big smiles on their faces. Azan returned the smile.

They sat around and talked and enjoyed being back together. But Azan could not help but feel devastated by the death of Jesus. "Father, why did he have to die? What should we do now that he is gone?"

Tears welled up in his eyes as he looked to his father for direction. "This cannot be all there is. I don't understand."

"I think the only thing we can do right now is to pray." He took Azan's hand and said, "Father God, please help us to know what to do, now that Jesus is gone from here. Give us strength to continue in his footsteps."

Azan added, "And Father God, thank you for answering my prayers for showing my father the truth about Jesus. I am so thankful. Amen"

Azan could not sleep that night and got up and went outside, overwhelmed by everything that had happened. He looked up into the starlit sky. *I can't imagine how devastated the disciples must be. I wonder where they are. God, please show us what we should do. I feel lost and scared. I don't understand why Jesus had to die. But I know you have a reason. Help me to understand.*

As the sun came up over the city, he saw people going about their usual business as if nothing had happened.

He said aloud, "Don't you understand that he was the long-awaited Messiah?"

Ephraim was standing next to him and heard him. He said to him, "There are those who may have missed it, but there are those of us who did not. We can hold the knowledge of Jesus in our hearts. God must have had a reason for Him to come and teach us and show us the miracles so we could believe in who he was and even for him to die. God's plans never fail. Do you believe this, Azan?"

"You're right, he must have a reason. We just don't know what it is yet!'

Azan and Ephraim decided to stay with the family at Ahava's house for the remaining time they would be in Jerusalem. Ephraim said to Amos and his family, "Thank you for your generosity in letting us stay here. I appreciate it very much."

"You're welcome here anytime. Come back again."

Ephraim said, "Goodbye, Eliana, I'll see you back in Capernaum."

"Okay, I will be here for another week and then I will return. Reuben and Maya will be coming back with us to visit Mother and Father."

Azan walked with his arm around Dobah's shoulder, holding on to Meir's hand, with Todros right next to them.

As they walked through the streets, they began to hear people talking excitedly. A woman was coming towards them, and they heard her shouting. "The tomb is empty! Jesus is not there! They stole his body, and no one knows where he is!" She continued through the streets, telling everyone.

Why would anyone steal his body? Wasn't it enough that they killed him?

Yosef hurried his family through the city to his sister's house. Once there, Yosef asked Ahava, "What have you heard about Jesus?"

She said, "They are claiming that Jesus' body is missing. There is talk about the disciples taking his body during the night. But the Romans were standing guard so this would not happen. Everyone is guessing what may have happened to him."

Just then, Medad and Eliah came in and said, "There are rumors that Jesus has risen from the grave. That he has appeared to the disciples. They say the curtain separating the Holy Place and the Most Holy place in the Temple was torn in two from top to bottom the moment that Jesus died. That when the earth shook, the rocks split, and the tombs broke open.

"They say the bodies of many holy people who had died were raised to life. They are reporting that they came out of the tombs after Jesus' resurrection and went into the holy city and appeared to many people. They said when the centurion and those with him who were guarding Jesus saw the earthquake and all that had happened, they were terrified, and exclaimed, 'Surely he was the Son of God!'"

They all looked at each other in wonder. Azan remembered what Jesus said the last time he heard him teach. "This is what Jesus said the last time I heard him teach in Capernaum."

'The reason My Father loves Me, is that I lay down My life only to take it up again. No one takes it from Me, but I lay it down of My own accord. I have authority to lay it down, and I have the authority to take it up again. This command
I have received of my Father.'

Is it possible that he *has* risen from the dead?

∼

It had been two weeks since Jesus died. People were still talking about what may have happened to him. As they were buying staples for the trip home, the merchant was talking to another man, who said, "The Pharisees want people to believe that his followers stole Jesus' body so the disciples could make it look like he rose from the grave. But I've heard that the disciples *have* seen him. They say Jesus *is* alive, and they have seen the wounds in his hands and feet. They said he even ate with them."

Azan said, "Wouldn't it be amazing if he has risen from the grave? Where are the disciples? We need to talk to them. I have so many questions. Didn't we see him die on the cross? We watched as they took him down and carried him off. Now they say he's alive! Wouldn't it be wonderful if this is true? He raised *others* that had died. He said, **'He has the authority to lay down his life and authority to take it up again.'"**

Eliah looked at the others. "Do you think this is true?"

Yosef said, "I don't know what to think about all of this. He is the Son of God. Anything is possible."

Azan got excited and said, "We must find the disciples. They will know if this is true or not. Let's hope they will return to Capernaum, and we can see them there."

Yosef called everyone together, "Let's discuss what we should do right now. We will stay in Jerusalem for another week or two to watch and see what happens. I will not be welcome back into the Synagogue when word gets back to Cana that I disagreed with the Pharisees. I made myself clear about how I feel about condemning an innocent man to death. Nor do I want to go back. They will persecute us for our belief in Jesus if we try to go back home. I am too well known in Cana. Ephraim and I talked, and we will go to Capernaum and decide from there what we should do. For now, Ahava has agreed that we can stay here until things settle down."

Ephraim spoke up and said, "You're welcome to stay with me. It might be a little crowded, but we can make it work."

Yosef said, "Then we all agree. I will go to Cana and sell the house and talk with Medad concerning the sheep and the vineyard. But first we will go to Capernaum."

Azan offered, "I'll go with you, Father."

Azan thought for a minute and then said, "You know, it's getting more difficult for Jonah to fish in his old age. His strength is failing him. Father, I have an idea. We can do the fishing and divide the proceeds of the catch with him for allowing us to use his boat. We can discuss it with him when we get back to Capernaum."

"Me, a fisher?" replied Yosef. "You will have a lot to teach me."

∾

A week passed, and they packed the donkey, said their goodbyes to Reuben and Ahava, and headed out of the city.

Azan was happy to have his family coming to Capernaum.

He enjoyed living there and had become close with Ephraim.

As they walked, Azan watched his father and Ephraim talking. *It's good to see them together.* Heba was walking with Galia, trying to keep Meir entertained. He was now seven, but he was still as energetic as ever.

Eliah, Todros, and Luke were walking together, talking.

Dobah was walking next to Azan as he pulled the donkey along.

She asked him, "Do you like living in Capernaum?"

"Yes, it's a nice town. People are friendly, and I have met some good friends there. You'll like it too. I can't believe how much you have grown up." *She is pretty, she looks like Mother; I will have to keep an eye on her.*

He watched Todros pull out the sling he had placed on his bed that night before he left Cana. He picked up a rock and shot it at a tree trunk. *That was me not too long ago. I guess I have changed; Jesus changed me. I want to do what pleases him. Jesus is kind, merciful, and forgiving, but most of all loving. I want to be like Jesus.*

He picked up a rock. "Todros, I challenge you to see who can shoot the farthest."

Todros handed the sling to Azan. He picked up a rock and shot it at the tree and missed. "I'm out of practice. Here you try, Todros."

He reached down and picked up a rock and put it in the sling, pulled it back, and let it go. It landed right in the middle of the tree trunk. Todros laughed aloud when he won.

"Todros, you have a good aim. I wasn't expecting that."

He noticed that Todros was walking a little taller. *I need to encourage him more. It's so good to be with my family again. I still can't believe what happened to Jesus, though.*

He prayed. *God, please give us direction for the next days, months, and years. I don't even know what to expect. Help me to know what the purpose was for Jesus' coming. And please let me see the disciples before too long. And thank you, again, for reconciling my father and I but mostly that he now believes in Jesus.*

CHAPTER 27

Back in Capernaum, Azan took Todros and showed him his loft. He said, "How would you like to share this space with me? We can put your bed up here with mine."

"Really, I can share this with you? This will be fun!"

Ephraim helped move things around in the house for the others. Ephraim seemed happy to have them. He had been alone for so long and now he was starting to let go of the grief he had been carrying.

Early the next morning, Azan and Yosef went to the shore and found Jonah's boat. Yosef said, "Show me what to do."

"You can start by putting the net into the boat." He walked over and tried to pick up the net and discovered how heavy it was.

"This is heavier than it looks." Azan just smiled. It had taken him a while to build the strength to lift it into the boat without struggling.

"Now I see how you got so strong."

"It has been good for me. Get in and I will push off."

Azan handed him a paddle, and they rowed out about a mile from shore. Azan said, "I want you to know that me being here in Capernaum was a good thing for me. I did miss you and

the family, but I have had good experiences here.

Ephraim has been great, and Jonah helped also."

"How did you meet Jonah and begin fishing with him?"

"After I left Cana, I met Jonah's son Andrew, and we walked to Capernaum together. Jesus called him and Andrew's brother

Peter to follow him. They are two of the twelve disciples that traveled with Jesus. Andrew asked me to help Jonah with his fishing business in his absence.

"I have spent time with Jesus and the others on occasion.

They were here in Capernaum often, and I was able to hear Jesus teach. He was humble and kind and helped people everywhere he went. He never turned anyone away."

Yosef said to him, "I am glad you were able to know him. You are not that young, naïve boy I once knew. I am immensely proud of who you have become."

"I hope the disciples come back to Capernaum soon. I cannot imagine what they are going through. They were remarkably close to Jesus. They spent three years with him, listening to him, growing to know him. I wish I could have spent more time with him. I have been writing down everything that I have seen and heard about him. I have it next to my bed. I wrote down everything that happened in Jerusalem last night after Todros fell asleep."

"I would love to read it sometime. Todros was so excited to sleep up there with you. He needs his big brother."

"Well, we're together now. God made it happen."

Back at the shore, they began unloading the fish and the nets when Jonah walked up. "Sorry I wasn't here this morning. I was a little tired and my day started slow. How did you do? I see you have a helper."

"Jonah, this is my father, Yosef."

"Nice to meet you."

"It's good to meet you also. Thank you for being so kind to my son."

"We were up early, and we needed time together. We didn't do too bad. About the normal catch. So, you know what happened to Jesus?"

"Yes, I was in Jerusalem right before he was arrested."

"So, you know that they crucified him and buried him?"

"Yes, I heard that his body had been stolen but then people were saying that he rose from the dead. I came home right after Passover. I have been waiting to hear from Peter and Andrew to see what they know."

Azan said, "I am hoping that they will return to Capernaum soon so we can talk to them. I have so many questions. My family and I have come back together, and they have moved here from Cana. I was wondering if you would like a break from fishing. I have seen how you sometimes struggle with the heavy work. I would like to suggest that my father and I could take over the fishing. We can split the proceeds of the catch with you for using your boat."

"You know, I was trying to think of a way for me to let go of the fishing. I am tired and you are right—my body is not as strong as it used to be. I like that idea."

"We can start soon, but first we need to go to Cana and settle our affairs there."

"Fine, you can start when you get back. Let's get these fish to market." They walked into the marketplace and found Amos at his booth. They exchanged the fish for their pay and talked for a while.

Jonah said, "I am handing over the fishing business to Azan and Yosef. They will pay me for the use of my boat, so you will have your dealings with them."

"Oh, that's good. You just mentioned how you wanted to retire the business. That works out great for me. I still have my supply."

The two headed back to the house, and Meir came running

when he saw them. Yosef scooped him up in his arms. "Did you go fishing? Did you catch any fish? How big were they?"

Yosef set him down, holding his arms out as far as he could.

"We caught one *this* big!" Meir's eyes grew big. "No, I am kidding you. We caught a bunch of smaller fish. Where is Mother?"

"She's in the house."

He went inside and said to her, "Azan and I will be going back to Cana day after tomorrow. Let me know what things you want us to bring back. We will take the donkey, and I will check with Ephraim to see if we can use his cart. We will have to part with things that are not necessary for us here."

She said, "There are only few things that are important to me. I would like the chest that father made for me prior to our wedding. I would like the items that are in the chest. Also, the rest of our clothes. Oh, and our winter clothes that I have stored in our room. I will need my sewing basket so I can continue to make things for the family. I especially want the bed covering that mother made for us. If you could bring some of the pots, bowls, utensils, and anything else that you have room for to cook with. The rest, you can dispose of or leave there."

They had been in Capernaum for only a couple of days, and it felt like home. Ephraim was enjoying Heba's help in the house. He made it known that he did not enjoy cooking and that he appreciated having his meals provided. He was able to spend more time in the shop and be more productive.

Azan spent time playing games with his siblings. He had made up games for the children in town to occupy them and now he shared them with Todros, Meir, and Dobah. They enjoyed connecting with each other again. He could hear his mother in the house singing as she worked. His heart was full, but he was still grieving Jesus' death.

At the table one night, they were just finishing eating when Ephraim said, "I have an announcement. You have met Eliana, Amos' sister. We have gotten to know each other, and I have become very fond of her. I have been grieving for so long, it has been nice to have the company of a woman again. I have met her father and mother and they are very upstanding people. I am going to ask for her betrothal."

Azan said, "I knew you two were getting close. Eliana is nice, and I'm glad you found her. I'm happy for you two."

Yosef said, "It is time for you to move on and find some happiness. I am pleased with your decision."

Heba added, "You have made an excellent choice. She is a wonderful person. When will you ask for her hand?"

"Within the next two weeks. We will have some time before we marry, but since I own my own house, we won't have to wait a full year."

"Well, we'll have to plan on being out of your home before that time arrives. I'm sure everything will work out."

Yosef said, "Azan and I can help fix the house up while we are here to make it nice for her. You have been on your own too long. It needs some cleaning up."

"Yes, I haven't been keeping it up all that well. I didn't see a need, but now I do."

Heba said, "This is cause for a celebration. We have Azan back with us, and we will be welcoming a new family member. We will have a celebration after you have asked for her hand. We'll invite her family to join us so we can meet them."

"That would be great." He was smiling from ear to ear. *Now I know why he has been walking with a spring in his step. I'm happy for him and Eliana. That will make us family with Amos, Hannah, and Luke. God, you have answered my prayers to bring my family back together and now you are growing it. Thank You!*

CHAPTER 28

Azan hugged his mother and told the children goodbye. He tugged at the reins to get the donkey moving, and the attached cart started rolling, bouncing over the rocks and bumps in the road.

The road to Cana was busy with travelers, and Azan thought as he walked along. *I'm sure glad this trip isn't four days long like the trip to Jerusalem. It will be odd to be back in the house I grew up in. It has been three years. I will miss being with Eliah, but I will invite him to come to Capernaum to go fishing.*

Yosef looked at Azan and smiled. "It's good to have you with me again. I missed you very much. We will have to work quickly to get things settled in Cana. I don't want to be there long. Besides, we have some work to do in Capernaum. We will have to prepare for a new family member. I'm happy for Ephraim. I was worried about him for a long time after his loss. He has isolated too long. You have been good for him. This was God's plan all along."

"It was. A lot of good has come from all of this. I just remembered something Jesus said to me. He said, '**You will have trouble in this life, but it will be for your good.**' *This* is what he meant. I want to understand what God's plan for

Jesus was about. He had to have a reason that he came, taught us, performed his miracles, and died. I guess we will know soon enough."

"God will reveal it to us in his time. We have only to trust."

∞

They arrived at the house and went inside. Azan looked around. *It does feel strange to be here. I remember the smell of mother's bread baking in the mornings and hearing the children playing outside, with Dobah calling out commands to her brothers, with them ignoring her.*

It was dusk, and Yosef suggested that they go wait at the sheep pen for Medad and Eliah, who were ushering the sheep in for the night. They sat by the old fig tree by the pen and talked.

"What are you going to do about the house, the vineyard, and the sheep?"

"I'm going to ask Medad to buy me out of the vineyard and the sheep. The house is another story. I will have to find someone who would take it over. I want to get a good price for it so we can use it to get set up in Capernaum. We'll get what we need from the house and leave the rest for the next person. They can disperse with the things they don't need or want. I want to have this done in just a couple of days."

"I hope Medad is open to this."

"I think he will be. He has a large family, and he may be able to get someone to go in with him. I just hope the fishing is sufficient for our keep."

"I have also learned a lot from Ephraim in the shop. I think between the two of us, we can make a good living."

They heard sheep and looked up to see them coming down the road.

Azan jumped up to go open the gate for them and the sheep funneled into the pen.

Eliah was bringing up the rear and shouted, "Azan, it is

good to see you again! Have you decided to come back here to Cana? I hope so!"

Azan replied, "That is a long story. We'll have to talk about it. Medad, good to see you!"

"Azan, I'm so glad you two are back together!"

YOSEF SAID, "We need to talk. Can we talk tonight after the meal?"

"Yes, I'm sure Galia and Heba would love to visit."

"Heba is in Capernaum with Ephraim and the children. It is just Azan and I."

"Oh, they didn't come back with you?"

"That is what we need to talk about."

"I am sure Gallia wouldn't mind if you ate with us. Come, let's go to my house."

Medad entered the house and announced to Galia, "Yosef and Azan are here."

She turned and saw them both, and she went over to Azan and hugged him. "I want you to know we have missed you. You have grown up so much! Look at you. You look healthy and strong, and you have grown about as tall as your father."

"I've been working, and it *has* made me stronger."

Medad asked, "Do we have enough for them to eat with us? They are here by themselves."

"Of course, please come sit and eat."

They all sat down while Galia finished putting the food on the table. When she finally sat down, she asked, "Are Heba and the other children in Capernaum?"

Yosef replied, "Yes, they stayed with Ephraim. We have decided to permanently move there. We came back to take care of things here. That is what I need to talk to Medad about."

After they ate, the boys went outside with the men and sat by the winepress. Medad started, "So, tell me what's on your mind."

"You know that I was troubled since I asked Azan to leave the house. I began to question everything I knew about our traditions, the law, about Jesus and about my relationship with my son."

"Yes, I've been concerned about you and the situation between the two of you."

"All this time, I have been researching the scripture and what it says about the law. I investigated who Jesus was, and over time, I realized that Azan was right all along about him being the Messiah." He looked at Azan and smiled.

"You believe that he is the Messiah?"

"I do now! I know they will kick me out of the synagogue for my new beliefs. That is why we are moving to Capernaum. I am too well-known here in Cana, and it would bring a hardship to my family for us to stay here. I want to sell you my half of the sheep and the vineyard. I know you can find another partner to take over my share."

"I understand your concerns. The Pharisees have been cracking down on anyone who even mentions Jesus' name, as you know. You are right, it would not go well for you here. I am sad to lose our partnership, but more so our friendship and daily activities together."

"You have always been a trusted friend, and that will never change. We came to disperse of our belongings and take care of the house. Would you consider buying me out of my half of the vineyard and the sheep? I also need to sell the house. Do you know of anyone who might be interested in it?"

"I have a cousin who is looking to move here and needs a place for him and his new wife. He would be a suitable candidate for taking up the business with me and the house would serve them well. I will send word to him about it.

"I will miss you and your family; we have been together for a long time. But I understand. We, too, believe that Jesus is the Messiah. I did not mention it to you because I thought I knew how you felt about it. I'm not involved with the Pharisees like you have been, and they have no interest in me. I don't think it will be a problem for us to stay here. At least for now."

Azan and Eliah talked the rest of the night about everything that had happened in the last three years. They were thankful to be together again. Azan said, "Eliah, you are welcome to come to Capernaum to visit any time you want. When you come to visit, we will go out fishing."

"I would enjoy that. I will visit as soon as I can."

∾

They spent the following day clearing things out of the house. They left items that could be of use to whoever moved in. They were careful to gather the things that Heba asked that they bring back. The items were mostly things that had meaning to her.

Yosef went into the room he shared with Heba. He was going through things and came across the book he had given to Azan for his Bar Mitzvah. He went to Azan, who was going through the things he had left behind.

"Azan, I want you to have this." He handed him the family book. He looked at it, and his eyes started watering.

"I gave it back to you. I didn't think I deserved it after disappointing you."

"I am not disappointed in you now, and I want you to have it. You are my son, and I will tell you again, I am proud of you.

You stood up for your convictions. I admire that about you."

"Thank you, I will treasure it."

They loaded what they were taking into the cart and left the house as neat as they could. Medad and Eliah came to the house and brought some skins of wine from the vineyard to take with them.

Yosef said, "I almost forgot to tell you that Ephraim is going to become betrothed to Eliana. You're invited to the wedding."

"That is wonderful. She is a good match for him. I hope they will be incredibly happy together. I'll let Galia know about it. I will be in touch with you about the house. I should hear from my cousin by next week. I will be in Capernaum at the beginning of the month for supplies. I will try to pay your shares by then."

"Thank you, Medad. You have been a good friend and partner. We'll see you next month."

"Eliah, plan to come out fishing when you come to Capernaum. We'll make a day of it."

"I look forward to it."

CHAPTER 29

A fter they got back to Capernaum, Azan took his mother
and Dobah to Amos' booth to buy food for the
house.

Amos was helping another patron. He looked up, and said,
"I'll be with you in moment."

Heba began looking through the vegetables. The patron
with Amos said, "You were gone for a while. Were you at the
Passover in Jerusalem?"

"Yes, my family and I went with some friends."

"So, you probably heard the rumors that Jesus had risen
from the dead."

"Yes, we heard that."

"Some believe it, and others think it is just a rumor. What
do you think?"

Amos looked up and saw a group of Pharisees approaching
them.

He tried to change the subject, "Yes, the figs are now out of
season. This is the last we will have this year—we won't have any
more till spring."

The man looked quizzically at him. Amos raised his head

and eyebrows slightly and motioned with his head to let the man know who was behind him. He turned and saw the Pharisees, and replied, "I guess the season *is* over for figs." They looked intently at Amos but kept walking. Once the Pharisees were out of hearing range, the man said, "Thank you for alerting me. They have been out a lot trying to catch people talking about Jesus. They know the disciples are back in Capernaum, and they want to keep things quiet."

"The disciples are here in town? Are you sure?"

"Yes, I saw them this morning, walking through the town center."

When Azan heard this, he looked at Heba and said, "Mother, I need to find them. Will you two be okay if I go?"

"Yes, I know the way back to Ephraim's. I hope you find them."

"Thanks, I'll be home later. I want to see what they have to say."

He ran to the shore to see if they were fishing. The boat was in its usual location, and no sign of the disciples. Then he ran to Jonah's house. He found Peter and Andrew with him.

"Azan, come in. We have things to share with you."

"And I have so many questions for *you*."

They were sitting at the table with Jonah, and they invited him to sit down.

"You were in Jerusalem for the Passover, and you know what happened to Jesus, right?"

"Yes, it was horrible. We saw everything they did to him. He was so brutally beaten that I could hardly recognize Him. We followed him through the streets and watched them nail him to the cross. It was excruciating to watch him suffer like that. I sat there the whole time until he took his last breath. They crucified him. I watched them take him off the cross after he died. They carried his lifeless body past me and took him to bury him!"

Peter and Andrew looked at each other and smiled.

Azan looked at them curiously and said, "*Why* are you smiling?"

Peter said, "Jesus is risen! We have seen him! He is alive!"

"You mean it's true? He *is* alive? But I saw them carry his body away. How can he be alive?"

"It's true," Peter said. "He appeared to me. Not only me, but Cleopas and another were walking to Emmaus and were talking about what had happened to Jesus. A man came up to them and asked what they were talking about.

"Cleopas asked him, 'Are you the only one who doesn't know the things that have happened in Jerusalem in these days?'

"*'What things?'* He asked.

"'About Jesus of Nazareth.' They told him that Jesus was a prophet, powerful in word and deed before God and all the people. The chief priests and rulers handed him over, an innocent man, to be crucified. But we had hoped that he was the one who was going to redeem Israel. And it is the third day since all this took place.

"Some of our women went to the tomb early this morning but didn't find his body. They came and told us that they had seen a vision of angels who said he was alive. We went to the tomb and found it just as the women had said, but they didn't see Jesus.'

"Then the man said, 'How foolish you are, and how slow to believe all that the prophets have spoken! Did not the Messiah have to suffer these things and then enter his glory?' He explained to them what the scriptures said concerning himself.

"It was late, and they asked him to stay with them, so he went in with them. When they were at the table, he took bread, gave thanks, broke it, and gave a piece to them. Then their eyes were opened, and they recognized him. It was Jesus and then he disappeared from their sight. They didn't recognize him in the beginning, but they said it was him.

"They asked each other, 'Were not our hearts burning within us while he talked with us on the road and opened the

Scriptures to us?' They at once returned to Jerusalem and found the eleven of us and those with us assembled. They told us, 'It's true! The Lord has risen and has appeared to us.'

"While we were still talking about this, Jesus himself stood among us and said, *'Peace be with you.'* We were frightened, we thought we saw a ghost. He said to us, *'Why are you troubled, and why do doubts rise in your minds? Look at my hands and my feet. It is I, myself! Touch me and see; a ghost does not have flesh and bones, as you see I have.'*

"We couldn't believe it. We were amazed. He asked if we had anything to eat. We gave him a piece of broiled fish, and he took it and ate it in our presence. Then he said, *'This is what I told you while I was still with you: Everything must be fulfilled that is written about me in the Law of Moses, the Prophets, and the Psalms.'*

"He opened our minds so we could understand the Scriptures. He told us, **'It is written;** *The Messiah will suffer and rise from the dead on the third day, and repentance for the forgiveness of sins will be preached in his name to all nations, beginning at Jerusalem.'* **"You are witnesses of these things. I am going to send you what my Father has promised; but stay in the city until you have been clothed with power from on high."** We were still together that same night and he appeared again and said, **'Peace be with you.'**

"He showed us his hands and feet and we were glad when we saw him. Again, he said, **'Peace to you! As the Father has sent Me, I also send you.'** Then He breathed on us and said to us, **'Receive the Holy spirit. If you forgive the sins of any, they will be forgiven them; if you retain the sins of any, they are retained.'**

"Thomas was not with us when Jesus came. When we told him we had seen Jesus, he said, 'Unless I see in His hand the print of the nails, and put my finger into His side, I will not believe.'

"After eight days, we were again inside, and Thomas was with us. Jesus came and stood before us and said, *'Peace to you!'* Then he told Thomas, *'Reach your finger here, and look at my hands; and reach you hand here and put it into my side. Do not be unbelieving but believing.'*

"Thomas answered and said to him, 'My Lord, and my God!' Jesus said to him, **'Thomas because you have seen me, you have believed. Blessed are those who have not seen and yet have believed.'"**

Peter went on to say, "We didn't understand what he meant when he said, *'On that day you will realize that I am in my Father, and you are I me, and I am in you.'*

"We now understand that he meant when he said, *'He who loves me, will be loved by my Father, and I too will love him and show myself to him. If anyone loves me, he will obey my teaching. My Father will love him, and we will come to him and make our home with him.'"*

They spent hours telling him about how Jesus came to fulfill the law in the scriptures. That they were in the upper room at Pentecost and how Jesus came to them and said, **'Receive the Holy Spirit.'** How they were now clothed with power from on high. They said that it was what Jesus had previously talked about. How this helped them understand everything that Jesus had taught them. How they saw him ascending into heaven.

My mind is racing after hearing all that Peter has said. Jesus has sent his Spirit to be in us. I remember learning from my studies at school that our God is One God. And Jesus saying that He and the Father are One. And here He is sending His Spirit. I am reminded of what I studied in Genesis about the Spirit at creation hovering over the waters. I believe that the Father, Son, and Spirit are One God. So much to think about.

Peter went on to say, "God has commissioned us to organize a church for ministry to preach the good news of the gospel to the entire world. Jesus died to forgive the sin of

CHILD OF THE KING

anyone who would believe that Jesus is the Son of God. The sins of believers have been forgiven; they will now have eternal life with Jesus."

Azan said, "I can hardly take all this in. So that's why Jesus came. I couldn't understand why he would come and then just die. I knew I was missing something."

Peter said, "He came to save us. To give us hope and eternal life. This is just the beginning."

"I am so amazed and excited that he's alive."

Andrew said, "That's what John the Baptist meant when he said, 'Behold! The Lamb of God who takes away the sin of the world!' He revealed Jesus to Israel. He also said, 'This is He who baptizes with the Holy Spirit.' He testified that Jesus was the Son of God."

Azan gasped and said, "I want to be baptized in the name of Jesus. Will you baptize me?"

Andrew, Peter, and Jonah looked at each other with smiles on their faces.

Peter said, "Tomorrow, meet us by the shore and we will baptize you."

Azan could not hold in his joy. "I must go tell the others. I will be at the shore in the morning!"

He ran as fast as he could and into the house, and though out of breath, tried to talk. "Jesus, Jesus *has* risen. He *is* alive! It's true!" Huffing, he said, "I just came from Peter and Andrew who told me everything. After three days in the tomb, he appeared to the disciples."

Yosef told him, "Slow down, we can't grasp what you are saying."

Azan caught his breath and said, "Peter and Andrew told me all these things. Jesus *is* alive, that he died to forgive us our sins. He came not to do away with the law but to fulfill it. They said he sent his Holy Spirit to help them remember everything he taught them.

He has commissioned them to spread the good news of the

Gospel. They are starting a church for ministry, so more people will become believers. Can you believe it? JESUS IS ALIVE!"

Yosef said, "This is hard to understand. You say they have seen him?"

"Yes, they've seen him several times. He showed them the nail marks in his hands and feet and the wound in his side. We *thought* God must have had a purpose for sending Jesus here. His purpose was for him to forgive our sins and to give us eternal life through his sacrifice on the cross. There is so much more to understand, but Peter said, 'We need to believe Jesus is the Christ, the Messiah, the Son of God.'

I have asked the disciples to baptize me. I want you all to be there. They are going to meet us at the shore tomorrow morning."

"Of course, we'll be there," Ephraim said.

∞

Azan, Yosef, Ephraim, Heba, and the children met beside Jonah's boat and waited there for Peter and Andrew. Soon all the disciples and Jonah came walking down to the shore, along with others who were following them.

Peter began preaching to all who were around. Azan was amazed at how boldly he was talking. He was on fire for the Lord. More people gathered around and listened to him. Then he went into the water and called Azan to him. Azan went to him, and Peter asked him, "Do you believe in the name of Jesus, that he came, died and rose again and that he is the Son of God?"

"Yes, I do believe in the name of Jesus and that he came, died, and rose again! I believe in the name of Jesus and that Jesus is the Son of God!"

Peter took him and laid him back into the water and lifted him up again, and said, "Repent, and be baptized in the name of Jesus Christ for the forgiveness of your sins." He drew Azan into him and hugged him. He then declared, "You are now a *Child of The King!*"

Peter then said to the crowd, "If you confess with your mouth that Jesus is Lord and believe in your heart that God raised him from the dead, you will be saved. For with the heart, one believes and is justified, and with the mouth one confesses and is saved."

After that, Yosef entered the water, and Peter baptized him.

One by one, his family entered the water. Peter baptized Heba, Ephraim, Dobah, Todros and even Meir. The other people witnessed this, and they came and asked Peter to baptize them.

Azan and his family gathered on the shore and praised God for all He had done and watched the others being baptized.

~

That night, they gathered around the table and broke bread and gave thanks to God, praising him with joy and gladness.

Azan prayed aloud, "Father God, thank you for sending Jesus to save us from our sins and to give us eternal life. I asked that you help me to understand why Jesus came and had to die. Thank you for helping me know that He came and lived and died for all of us. To forgive our sins. He is King! And I am a *child* of the *One True King!*

I am proclaiming to you all that I want to help the disciples in spreading the good news. I want to be part of starting the church. I want to serve in this mission." He started dancing around the room, declaring, "Jesus is alive. He's alive.

"I'm a child of the King!"

CAN YOU HELP?

Thank You For Reading My Book!
Please leave me an honest review on Amazon letting me know
what you thought of the book.

Thanks so much!
K. G. Ingram

NOW IT'S YOUR TURN

Discover the EXACT 3-step blueprint you need to become a bestselling author in as little as 3 months.

Self-Publishing School helped me, and now I want them to help you with this FREE resource to begin outlining your book!

Even if you're busy, bad at writing, or don't know where to start, you CAN write a bestseller and build your best life.

With tools and experience across a variety of niches and professions, Self-Publishing School is the only resource you need to take your book to the finish line!

DON'T WAIT

Say "YES" to becoming a bestseller:

https://self-publishingschool.com/friend/

Follow the steps on the page to get a FREE resource to get started on your book and unlock a discount to get started with Self-Publishing School

ABOUT THE AUTHOR

THE MOST IMPORTANT TITLE I HAVE IS "CHILD OF THE ONE TRUE KING."

Through God's inspiration, this book came to be.
I am simply one who trusts in the Lord Jesus Christ.
I will confine my boasting not to what I have done,
but what God has done through me.

"Jesus is the author and perfecter of our faith."
Hebrews 12:2

K. G. Ingram

Made in the USA
Las Vegas, NV
15 August 2023

76137470R00114